Fly Tying
with A. K.

Fly Tying
with A. K.

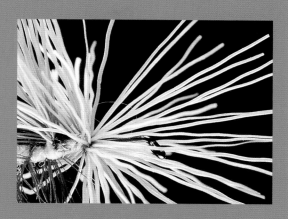

Patterns and Problem Solving
with New Materials and Techniques

A. K. BEST

STACKPOLE
BOOKS

Published by
STACKPOLE BOOKS
5067 Ritter Road
Mechanicsburg, PA 17055
www.stackpolebooks.com

Printed in China

First edition

10 9 8 7 6 5 4 3 2 1

Photography by A. K. Best
Cover design by Wendy A. Reynolds

Library of Congress Cataloging-in-Publication Data

Best, A. K., 1933–
    Fly tying with A.K. : patterns and problem solving with new materials and techniques / A.K. Best. — 1st ed.
        p.   cm.
    Includes index.
    ISBN-13: 978-0-8117-0375-8
    ISBN-10: 0-8117-0375-4
    1. Fly tying. I. Title.

SH451.B457   2008
688.7'9124—dc22
                                                                2007046657

To my wife, Jan,
whose love and patience seem endless.

Contents

Preface

It seems that each new year brings with it new challenges we fly fishers and fly tiers need to face. These days it's bird flu and the impending fear of an international human pandemic that could decimate the populated world as we know it. Underlying that, to those of us in the fly-fishing world, is the fear that there will be damn few birds that we can continue to use for tying flies. I doubt the major producers of fly-tying feathers will be affected, but it could happen. And what about all the imported feathers that have become such a staple in the fly tier's inventory of materials? The U.S. government has already placed embargoes on poultry products from certain countries. It's a concern that I have been trying to deal with in regard to strung Chinese rooster neck hackle, for example. If I have a signature fly, it's the Quill Body Fly. I found a replacement material that is even better than the original rooster quill, which I explain in chapter 9.

Another challenge we need to face is how to manipulate new materials. Many of the old rules in fly tying are no longer applicable simply because new replacement materials for tailing and hackling cannot be attached to the hook the way it's always been done. The old rules, formulated some two hundred years ago, were devised to allow tiers to create good flies by using the materials the way they demanded. Hackling a dry fly is an excellent example. Dry-fly necks of a hundred years ago contained shorter feathers than we see today, and they were basically flat from the quill to the hackle tips. Dry-fly necks being produced today have a greater hackle density and are much longer than anyone could have dreamed of even fifty years ago. Today's neck hackle is still basically flat, but many of the dry-fly saddles have cupped hackles, fibers that are curved toward the concave or dull side of the feather. Both the increased hackle density and the cupping effect have dramatically altered the manner in which I now hackle dry-fly duns and parachutes. You can avoid trapped hackles!

I teach a lot of fly-tying classes during the winter months each year, and from those classes I learn some things that cause many of the students big problems in getting materials tied onto the hook the way they would like. I addressed hand position in my book, *Advanced Fly Tying* (Lyons Press, 2001). Equally important is the problem of the bobbin hand, for it is often the angle of the thread in relation to the angle of the bobbin tube and how you hold the bobbin in the hand that can cause or solve problems in fly tying.

New materials, new techniques, new patterns, and pattern alterations are the nub of this book. I hope the material herein will help solve some problems you may be having.

Problem-Solving Techniques

CHAPTER 1

The Bobbin Hand

A lot of information has been written about how to hold materials on the hook when tying flies. Someone must have said something about the bobbin hand in the instructions on how to tie a particular fly, but I can't remember seeing much of it anywhere. It is very important to hold materials in just the right spot and at just the correct angle before winding tying thread over them, but equally important is what you do with the bobbin hand (and the bobbin) after the materials are where they're supposed to be.

I've been teaching fly-tying classes across the continent for almost twenty-five years and have seen a lot of problems caused by the bobbin hand. Most tiers can place the materials onto the hook correctly, but when they try to wind the thread around the hook shank and the materials, everything goes to hell. I'm beginning to think that what you do with the bobbin hand and bobbin might be more important than how you hold the materials.

The mistakes I have seen include one tier who had a very expensive bobbin but held it in such a manner that he didn't need it! In other words, he used his forefinger and thumb to guide the thread, not the end of the bobbin tube, which was hidden someplace behind the thumb and forefinger pads. Many tiers have six to ten inches of thread between the end of the bobbin tube and the hook shank. Some use only the forearm when winding the thread. Few tiers understand how the angle of the bobbin tube to the thread and the angle of the thread to the hook can dramatically increase accuracy of thread placement and make tighter thread wraps. Another error is the tendency to always use tension on the thread when making the first turn. All of these things will create some kind of trouble, either when you begin the fly or just before you finish.

It doesn't matter what kind of bobbin you use, it's where you place the end of the tube where the thread comes out that is most important. I prefer the old-style S & M bobbin (by the way, Wasatch is now selling S & M bobbins with ceramic inserts!) because of their heavier weight. Most tiers use the open-frame bobbin, such as the Matarelli. In either case, there is one correct way to hold the bobbin, as shown in the photos below. If you can become accustomed to holding the bobbin in such a way as to expose only about half an inch of bobbin tube, you'll gain complete control of where the thread goes when you wind it around the hook. Holding the bobbin in this way puts the spool near the heel of your hand and allows you to use your fourth or fifth finger for controlling thread tension by applying pressure to the spool with either or both finger pads.

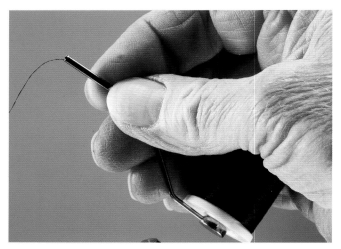

Holding a Matarelli bobbin

You only need about half an inch of thread between the end of the bobbin tube and the hook shank. If you have more than that, you begin to lose control of exactly where the thread goes as you wind it onto the hook and over the material. By exactly where it goes, I'm talking about the difference of one thread width to the left or right over the material. Have you ever wondered how people who tie those beautiful classic married-wing Atlantic salmon flies are able to do that? It's a simple matter of perfect thread control.

Here's how to gain perfect thread control: Begin by shortening the amount of thread between the end of the bobbin tube and the hook shank, as shown in the photo below.

Holding an S & M bobbin

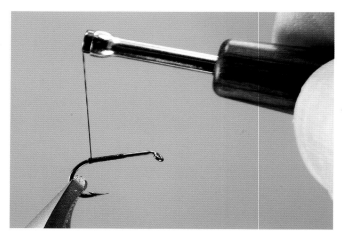

Short thread

Place a segment of material, such as a clump of tailing fibers for a dry fly, on the hook by laying the clump against your side of the hook and at about a 45-degree angle to the hook shank. At this point you simply cannot tie the clump onto the hook and have it go where you want (exactly on top of the hook) with a tight thread. You must allow a little slack in the thread in order to place it where you want, and then quickly tighten it. If you have more than half an inch of thread between the end of the bobbin tube and the hook shank, you will have to keep the thread under tension to make it go where you want. Tension on the thread will always spin the material out of position. An annoying thing often happens at this point: The little loop of thread wants to fall forward, and no matter how hard you try, it won't go where you want, which should be exactly over the last wrap of thread on the hook shank under the tailing fibers. The fix is simple: Spin the bobbin in a counterclockwise direction to put some twists in the thread, and it will fall to the rear. The following photo demonstrates a loose loop that wants to fall forward, and the next photo shows how the loop will fall to the rear after spinning the bobbin.

It's important to remember that you can gain control of where the loop goes only by having a very short amount of thread between the bobbin tube and the hook.

You will also be able to gain more thread control if you practice using just your fingers and wrist to wind thread around the hook. I see a lot of tiers using only the forearm, with no wrist or finger flexibility. The following series of photos demonstrates tying a dubbed-body parachute pattern to illustrate what I'm talking about. Notice that each photo shows very little forearm movement. I'll begin with the example of winding thread forward around the butts of the tailing material after it has been anchored when tying a dry fly, as demonstrated in the three previous photos.

Thread vertical

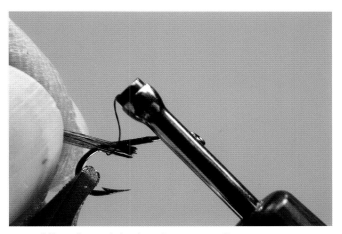

Loop falling forward (with tailing material)

Thread going around and away

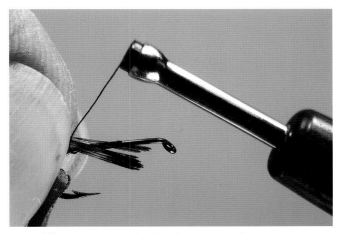

Loop falling to the rear (with tailing material)

Thread coming down

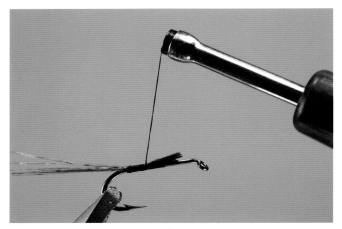

Thread coming up and forward

Thread back to vertical

Notice that except in the second and fourth photos above, the angle of thread to hook shank is nearly 90 degrees, which indicates that the thread is leaning slightly forward. This is because the axis of the rotation is actually in the wrist, coupled with some movement of the fingers.

Step two in tying a parachute pattern is to attach material for the post. I always use white turkey T-base segments for all my parachutes. It's white and a hell of a lot easier and faster than trying to stack calf body or calf-tail hair, which has been the traditional material for parachute posts. Besides, I'll bet there isn't a trout anyplace on the planet that knows the difference. By the way, white turkey T-base is a short, two- to three-inch-long feather that is almost straight along its tip and has very little fringe at the fiber tips. Most fly shops label these as turkey flats. That's wrong. Turkey flats come from the back or saddle portion of the bird, are six to eight inches long, and are no good for use as wing posts on parachutes because of the length of the fringe at the end of each fiber. Turkey T-base comes from the neck and breast of the bird.

Turkey flat

Turkey T-base

The quickest way I have found to use a T-base feather is to first clip out the center quill for a distance that is equal to the hook-shank length.

Clipping out center quill

Then fold back the fibers on each side of the quill until each of the remaining halves are equal to the hook-shank length. Do not strip off the fibers. You may have enough left on the remaining feather for another wing post.

Folding fibers back

Fold the two halves together to make one clump. This clump becomes an instant wing post.

Wing post

Measure the wing post to be a long as the hook shank, and place it against your side of the hook shank, about two hook-eye spaces behind the eye at a 45-degree angle with the tips below the hook.

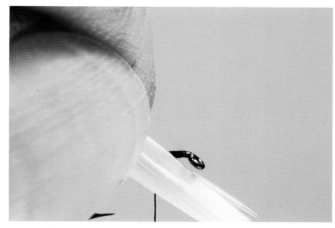

Wing clump in place

Take one loose turn of thread over the hook and post material. Gradually tighten the thread as you come up and around the hook for a second turn. Be certain that the second turn of thread is precisely in front of the first, and use the second turn of tight thread as a push bar to torque the post material around to the top of the hook.

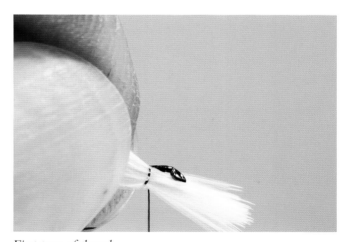

First turn of thread

Second turn of thread, post material on top of hook

Make the third turn of thread to come up and around *behind* the first turn of thread.

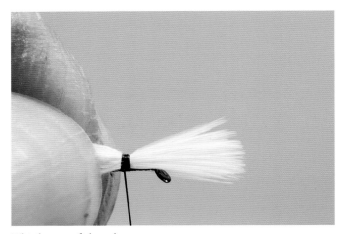

Third turn of thread

Continue with very firm turns of thread behind the third until you have at least seven turns of thread. Then lift the butt of the feather and lay your scissors horizontally to clip off the butt. This will create an angled cut, which is easier to cover with two or three more turns of thread. It is much easier to taper body material over a tapered post butt than if it's clipped off vertically.

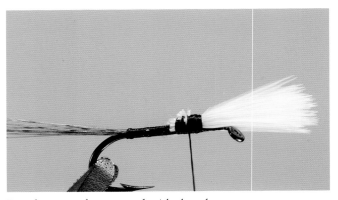

Parachute post butt covered with thread

Bring the thread forward so that it's immediately in front of the post. Lean the post to the rear, and create a thread dam in front of it to make it stand perpendicular to the hook. It's very important that you maintain a thread angle as shown in the photo below to achieve a thread dam that doesn't take up much space in front of the post. Ten or eleven turns of thread should be enough.

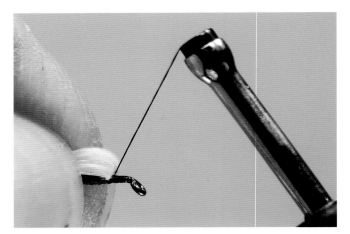

Thread angle for making thread dam

The next step is to thread wrap the base of the post. This is most crucial if you want to avoid problems winding a hackle around it later. The base of the post must be very firm.

Bring the tying thread up and around the post as close to the top of the hook shank as possible. Take one complete turn of thread, grip the tips of the wing post with your materials hand, and pull straight away on the tying thread to firmly gather all the fibers. The amount of tension you apply should be near the breaking point of the thread. Make the turn of thread, tighten, and give it a couple more little tugs just to make sure the base is completely compressed. Release the post tips and continue winding thread up the post until you have enough of a thread base to accommodate the number of hackle turns you'll need.

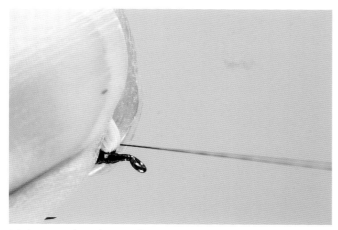

Tightening thread around wing post

Thread base on wing post

I always apply a drop of head cement to the base of the post before continuing.

Applying a small drop of lacquer to wing post base

Construct the body of the fly with either dubbing or a quill, and leave the thread to hang down immediately in front of the wing post.

Tying on the hackle butts requires exact placement of the thread wraps as well as holding the hackle quills in the correct position. This is true for both standard hackled duns and parachutes. (See chapter 4, "Avoiding Trapped Hackles.")

Which brings me to explain how to hold the bobbin while executing a hand whip-finish, or using a whip-finish tool if you want a good, tight knot. The thread coming out of the bobbin *must be parallel to the hook shank and as close to it as possible!* I see many tiers hold the bobbin off to one side as they whip-finish. This will cause the thread to be some distance away from the area immediately behind the hook eye. And it absolutely prevents the first turn of thread around the bobbin thread and the hook from becoming completely tight. The next photo demonstrates this common fault in finishing the head, which will come loose.

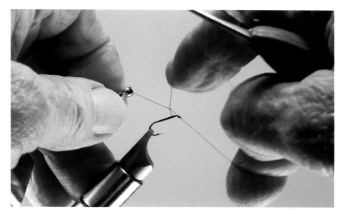

First turn of an incorrectly done whip-finish creating a loose turn

The next photo shows where the thread and bobbin should be when making a whip-finish knot.

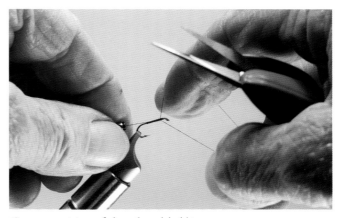

Correct position of thread and bobbin

If you are having trouble with breaking the thread while tightening, such as when making the first turn around a parachute post or spinning deer hair, always pull directly away from the hook shank with the bobbin tube directly in line with the thread. The thread will break more easily if the bobbin tube is at a right angle to the thread. The following two photos demonstrate the right and wrong ways to tighten thread.

Wrong way to tighten thread (thread and bobbin in down position for clarity)

Right way to tighten thread

One of the most important uses of the bobbin hand is in controlling thread torque. What I mean here is what happens to the material that you are tying onto the hook after you apply some thread tension. I can't think of a single instance when thread torque does not move the material to some degree. Everyone ties flies using varying amounts of thread tension at each step, so it's impossible to use a term that would indicate a certain number of pounds or ounces of tension that a tier should use at any time. My goal is to tie every thing onto the hook with thread tension that is just under the breaking point of the thread I'm using for a particular fly. The only way you're going to learn that is to keep applying tension to your tying thread until it breaks. More tension will always result in more torque and increased movement of the material you're tying to the hook.

The best way to learn about thread torque and material movement is to place the material you're about to use on top of the hook, place the thread with the short-thread loose-loop technique, quickly tighten it, and watch to see how far the material moves. If it moves from a 12:00 position to a 2:00 position, then simply place the material at a 10:00 position, and after the thread has been tightened, the material should be exactly on top of the hook. It's always best when placing most materials on the hook to be certain that the material is touching the hook shank and at about a 45-degree angle to the shank before making the first turn of thread. (Thorough discussions of quill segment tails and wings appear in corresponding chapters in my book *Production Tying,* 2nd ed., Pruett Press, 2003.) The following series of photos demonstrates the above.

Many tiers place winging material, such as hen hackle tips, on top of the hook and attempt to tie them down and have them stay in that position. It hardly ever works out the way the tier intends. This is demonstrated in the following two photos.

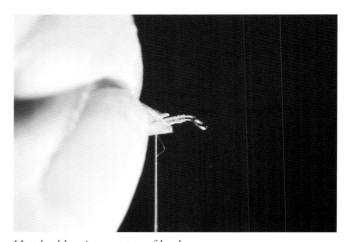

Hen hackle wings on top of hook

Position of wings after tightening thread

Hen wings on top of hook after thread tightening

The best way to accomplish tying hen hackle tip wings onto the hooks is to place the wing butts so that they straddle the hook at an angle of about 45 degrees to your side of the hook. Take one turn of thread over the butts, and then, as you make the second turn of thread over the butts, roll your grip to the top of the hook and pull back slightly. This will always put the wings directly on top of the hook. See the following two photos.

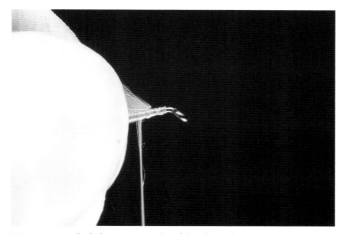

Hen wings slightly to one side of hook and at an angle

It simply involves a basic understanding of physics. Use thread torque as your friend instead of treating it as an enemy. I normally use about a 10:30 position for tying tailing materials, biots, hen wings, and parachute wing posts to the hook. The first turn of thread anchors the material, and the second turn of thread acts as a push bar to aid thread torque in moving the material to the top of the hook.

And you must be aware that, as in all things made by man or machine, there will be sections in any spool of thread, whether it's prewaxed single-strand floss, 4/0, 6/0, 8/0, or smaller, that are weaker than the rest of the spool. The best thing to do when you find such an area is to pull off about six feet of thread, cut it off, and begin again. Another thing to remember is that the folks who manufacture fly-tying threads run thousands of spools of a single strength in a single color at one time. The spools are boxed and put on a shelf for shipment when their orders come in. If the last box of black 6/0 was made two years ago, when you buy it you'll probably have a weaker thread than if it were new. It also depends on how your retailer displays tying threads. If the display is near a window, go someplace else to buy your thread, because the sun will have had a chance to begin destroying it.

Spinning deer or elk hair requires a mastery of the art of controlling thread placement and torque. Some tiers have told me they use 6/0 or even 8/0 thread when spinning deer hair. I've never understood the reason why one would do that, since the thread is never visible on the finished fly. I always use Danville's monocord as the minimum-strength thread when spinning deer or elk hair, because I want to spin it onto the hook as firmly as possible. Besides the extra strength of monocord, it's also a little wider and therefore doesn't cut into the individual hairs as easily as finer threads when I tighten it. Once again, the thread placement is mandatory, as demonstrated in the following photos.

Tying A. K.'s Hopper

You must have a bare hook shank to successfully spin deer or elk hair. I'll use the example of a hopper pattern I call A. K.'s Hopper. It's basically a Joe's Hopper body combined with a Letort wing and a Whitlock head. The directions begin after the body and wing have been tied on, ready to spin the head.

1. Select a hair patch that contains large-diameter hair. Snip off a segment that is about the same diameter as three wood kitchen matches. Comb out all the underfur and clip away the tips until you have a segment of hair butts about one inch long. The butts of the hair will be more buoyant and will flare readily. Place the clump on top of the hook with the butts to the rear and take two loose turns of thread.

2. Gradually add tension to the thread as you continue winding it to make a third turn. Do not release your grip on the hair butts until you see the hair beginning to flare.

3. Release the hair butts and continue winding thread in exactly the same spot as the first two turns, with increasing tension. The hair should spin completely around the hook on the fourth turn of thread.

4. Work the thread forward through the clump on the fifth turn.

5. Be sure the thread is now in front of the spun hair, then stroke it back forcefully with your materials hand thumb and forefinger, and take two turns of thread directly in front of the hair clump. This anchors the clump in place and prevents it from loosening.

6. Continue spinning hair clumps until you run out of space to put more. After the second or third clump, you should use a hair packer to condense the spun hair clumps as tightly as you can. Make certain that the last clump of hair is spun on with the butts forward over the eye. This will provide a crisper-looking head after it has been trimmed.

Another pesky problem that can be solved with correct thread placement is what to do about those little stray fibers after tying on hen hackle spinner wings. It's often close to impossible to snip out those little fibers without cutting off some of the wing. In fact, you can solve two problems at the same time. Hen hackle wings also tend to take a folded-back set after a few casts. This is not the fault of the material, and you can prevent it in the following manner. Tie the hen hackle wings on as usual, then separate and flatten them to their horizontal position. There always seem to be some stray fibers at the base of each wing that can get caught up in the figure-eight thorax dubbing and look bad when the fly is finished. The only remedy at this point is to carefully snip them away with your scissor points. Here's how to solve both problems:

Controlling Stray Fibers

1. Do not begin to build a thorax using the figure-eight method. Instead, bring the tying thread to hang immediately behind the wings and carefully build the thinnest dubbing rope on the thread that you possibly can.

2. Capture stray fibers with dubbing rope.

3. Complete rear doughnut.

4. Build a dubbing/thread dam immediately behind the wings with about six or seven turns of thread. Capture the stray fibers behind the wing with the thin dubbing rope as you do this. Try to build up what amounts to a tiny doughnut of dubbing behind and against the wings.

5. Doughnut in front of the wings: Bring the tying thread forward beneath the wings to hang down immediately in front of the wings. Note that there are no stray fibers at the front or rear of the wings! Repeat step 2.

6. Both front and rear doughnuts with thin dubbing rope: Add more dubbing to the thread, but keep it as thin as before.

7. Wrap dubbing behind rear doughnut.

8. Wrap dubbing in front of front doughnut.

9. Begin to figure-eight wrap the thorax area, being extremely careful to keep each wrap on the outside edge of both doughnuts. No turn of dubbing rope should touch either wing. This will compress each doughnut against the wings and prevent them from taking a delta wing set after a few casts.

You may wonder how such minor differences in thread placement can be important. Especially when you examine some of the photo sequences. All of this is stuff I have learned by tying thousands of dozens of flies and trying new ways to solve problems. Much of that comes down to absolute thread control, tension, torque, and bobbin handling. These are the methods that have worked for me.

CHAPTER 2

Cutting Things Off

You can do everything right, have the right tools, top-drawer materials, good lighting, excellent thread control and bobbin angles, and enthusiasm for tying, but still occasionally wonder why your flies don't look the way you want. Somehow they just look a little scraggly, maybe even a little bulky. Many times this is caused by how you cut things off after you've tied them onto the hook. And it begins with the first thing you do when you sit down to tie a fly.

Most fly-tying instructions begin with a statement about attaching the thread to the hook, winding to the beginning of the bend, and cutting off the thread tag. There are a couple of ways to do this without leaving a short, ugly, fuzzy tag of thread sticking up when you're done. It's almost impossible to get rid of this once it's there. You can always try to cover it up with materials added later, but this doesn't always work, because this maneuver often extends the body down into the hook bend, displacing the tailing downward—or worse yet, crowding the head space. The best thing to do is leave no tag end.

One method of making sure there is no fuzzy thread end is to cut the tag off a few turns before you get to the bend of the hook. It's a good way, but you lose the option of using the thread tag to guide the last few turns of thread. It will slow you down as you try to keep each turn of thread tightly nested against the previous one.

A second option is to give the tag a quick tug toward the hook eye and snap it off where it comes off the hook. It's my favorite method. But you have to be a little careful how you do this. The last turn of thread around the hook and over the tag must be held against the hook very tightly, with the thread going away from you or straight down. The tight thread coming from the bobbin essentially cuts off the tag as you quickly tug it forward.

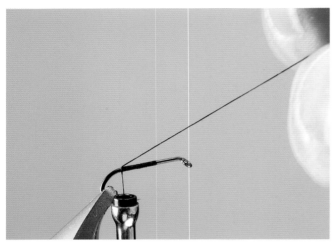

Thread in position for snapping off the tag

Then give the thread tag a quick yank forward, and the tight thread on the hook will cut off the tag.

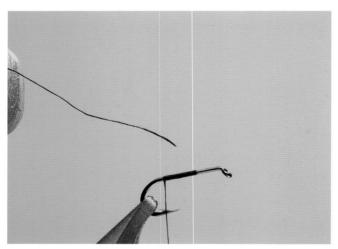

Separated tag and no stub

A third method to remove the tag is to slice it off with an open scissor blade. Wiss scissors are marvelous for this use, as the blades are razor sharp. Simply hold the thread tag at about a 45-degree angle above the hook shank, lay the open scissor blade horizontally behind the thread tag, and slice forward. The last two or three tight turns of thread over the tag will roll over the sliced-off tag. It's the same technique that rod wrappers use to slice off their tags when wrapping guides on a rod.

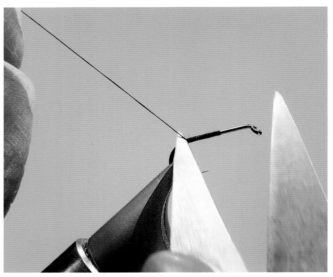

Slicing off thread tag with Wiss scissors

The best way to avoid material tags, stubs, and tufts is to cut them off before you tie them on. This is especially true with quills, yarn, tinsels, braids, and dry-fly hackle butts. I've seen dozens of photos included in fly-tying instructions that demonstrate a piece of material that has been tied to the hook with a long piece of butt section or tip that must be snipped off after it has been tied down. It always leaves a stub of something sticking out. I have always figured if I have to cut it off anyway, why not cut it off ahead of time? It's usually better to cut the material, place it on the hook, take a couple turns of thread to anchor it, and then pull the material back slightly until its end is under the thread turns. The end of the material becomes invisible. The following series of photos demonstrates the difference between cutting something before and after it has been tied on.

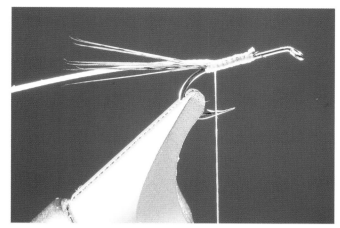

Quills tied on, then trimmed

Yarn segment trimmed, then tied on

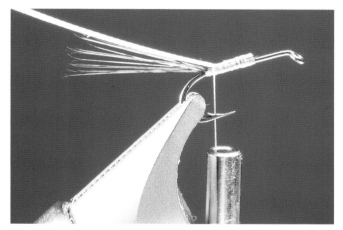

Quills tied on after trimming

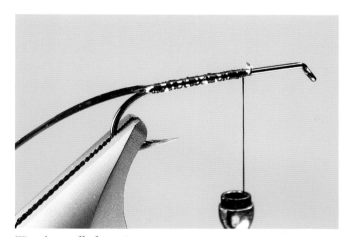

Tinsel cut off after tying on

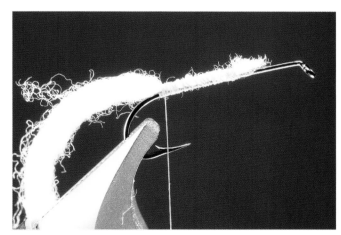

Yarn segment tied on, then trimmed

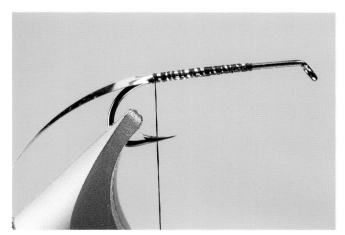

Tinsel tied on after cutting

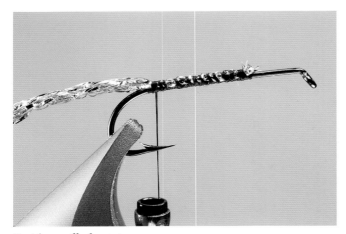

Braid cut off after tying on

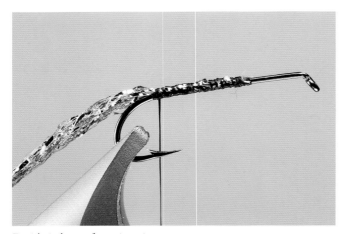

Braid tied on after trimming

Hackle butt trimmed after tying on

Hackle butt tied on after trimming

Some of the problems of cutting things off without leaving ugly and unmanageable stubs sticking out can be solved by using the scissors at the correct direction and angle. See the photo on page 20 for an excellent example. If the scissors come toward the hook from the side of the hook, there will always be a longer stub on the yarn segment. Cutting off the butt of a parachute wing post to create a smooth junction over which to wrap body material as described in chapter 1 is also very important.

On some fly patterns, you do not want to use a tapered cut for the body material. One that comes to mind is my hopper pattern that I used as an example in chapter 1. It is absolutely essential that the yarn body shoulder be perfectly vertical. If there is the slightest taper, the whole wing assembly will slide forward and come loose. There's also the nagging little problem of the turkey wing segment splitting as it is tied on. This can be prevented to some degree by liberally spraying the turkey feather with Krylon Workable Fixatif before cutting out the individual segments. What really causes the segment to split, however, is the manner in which the palmered hackle is cut off after it has been wound. Tying this fly requires a lot of thinking ahead to what happens next. Carefully study the following photo series to learn the method of creating an abrupt vertical shoulder and how to tie off and trim a palmered hackle.

Vertical Shoulders and Palmered Hackles

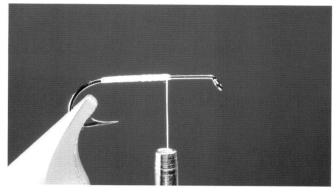

1. Start the tying thread one hook-gap space behind the eye. Save this amount of bare hook shank for spinning the deer-hair head later. Wind the thread to the end of the bend, snip off the tag, and return the thread to the starting point.

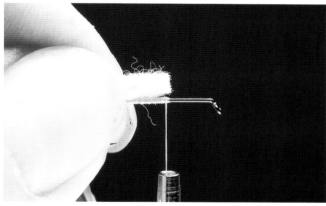

2. Be certain that the end of the yarn to be tied onto the hook has been cut perfectly square. If there is the slightest taper here, you're out of luck for what comes next!

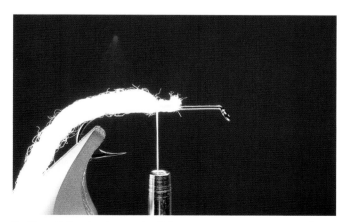

3. Carefully tie the end of the square-cut yarn exactly on top of the first turn of thread behind the hook eye. Make

the thread turns as close as possible to the end of the yarn, but leaving the tiniest tuft visible. Take six or seven very firm turns of thread.

4. Tightly spiral-wrap the thread over the yarn to the end of the shank, and make seven very firm turns of thread over the last turn.

5. Twist the yarn to create a short extended body loop, and tie the loop down with six more very firm turns of thread.

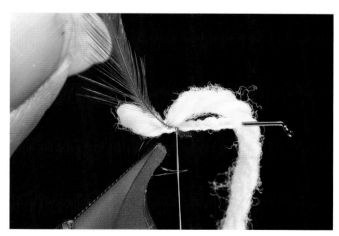

6. Fold the remaining yarn back, and tie in the butt of a saddle hackle on your side of the hook and in front of the loop, with its shiny side to the rear.

7. Fold the hackle back and begin winding the yarn forward. When you get to the tie-off spot for the yarn, bring it up and around to the top of the original yarn tie-down. Tie the yarn down slightly to the far side of the hook. Make five or six extremely firm turns of thread over the exact same spot as the tie-down shown in the photo accompanying step 3.

8. The next step is most important. Fold the remaining yarn segment to the rear, and place the scissor tips in line with the hook shank as shown in the photo.

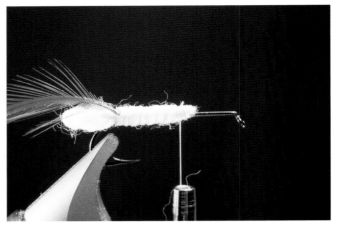

9. This is the only way to produce an absolutely vertical shoulder upon which you need to tie a turkey wing segment and a sparse deer-hair overwing. And it is also essential that not much space be used for the addition of these two materials, since the trimmed deer-hair head won't be able to hide all the tie-downs unless they are kept very close to the end of the body.

10. Wind the hackle forward in open spiral turns, trying to get the hackle quill to seat between the turns of yarn to protect the quill from trout teeth. When you get to the front (shoulder) of the body, continue winding the hackle around to the far side of the body, where you tie it down with only two or three turns of thread. (The hackle tip will be firmly anchored later, when the turkey segment and sparse hair wing are tied on.) Snip off the hackle stem on the far side of the hook. This will prevent a hackle stub from poking through the turkey quill segment and splitting it as you tie it down.

11. Tie on the turkey segment.

12. Tie on the sparse deer hair.

CHAPTER 3

Preventing Body Bumps

Many of the flies I see in fly shops, fly fishers' fly boxes, at some fly-fishing shows, even in some photos that accompany advertisements and, surprisingly, magazine articles and the occasional book have bumps where there shouldn't be any. I know the fish couldn't care less about it, but when I see those examples, I tend to wonder how well the rest of the fly is tied. Fly tying requires absolute attention to detail. Why not eliminate a flaw?

We all begin with a bare hook and some thread that we use to hold things firmly to the hook. There is always a technique to use to attach the materials solidly to the hook in such a way that it's not obvious to the viewer. In most instances, the attachment of the initial material is covered by the application of the next piece. A good example is tailing and then body materials on most flies. You must be very careful, however, to cover the last turn of thread with body material at the point where the tailing extends from the hook shank. It's a small thing, and something I don't always pay close attention to when I'm hurriedly tying half a dozen flies for myself at camp. Then, sometime later, when I'm searching through my fly box for a fresh fly, I'm always a little dismayed when I see that last turn of thread holding the tailing in place, and I wonder if I tied the rest of the fly in such a sloppy fashion.

Most novice to intermediate tiers try tying streamers early on in their sessions at the vise. I think that's because everything is bigger and a little easier to handle. Since everything is bigger, it's easier to spot mistakes and fix them. (You can only make little mistakes on little flies!) Following are a couple of things you can do to eliminate body bumps and exposed thread on streamers.

Streamer Techniques

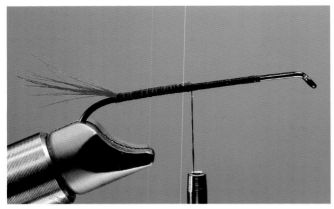

1. If the streamer pattern calls for a small clump of red hackle for the tail, you are in trouble before you begin, since it's almost impossible to find hackle fibers long enough to go all the way up the hook shank to within a hook-gap space behind the hook eye unless you are tying a very small streamer. And if that's the case, you might consider a soft-hackle wet fly instead. I think of streamers as flies that are tied on hook sizes from 8 to 2 using a Mustad 79580 as the standard streamer hook length. Tying a hackle fiber tail on hooks this size will always leave a small bump someplace in the middle to upper third of the body, since the material isn't long enough.

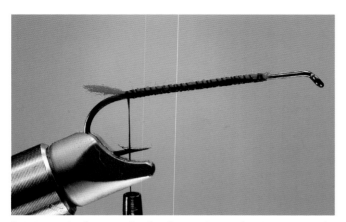

2. Use a single strand of red yarn instead. Tie it onto the hook about a hook-gap space behind the hook eye, lash it down to within half a hook-eye space short of the end of

the shank, and clip it off to a length that is equal to the distance from the hook point to the end of the barb. Stopping the tailing tie-down just short of the end of the hook shank will eliminate the possibility of any of the thread wraps over the tailing from peeking out when you wind on the body material. I tie streamer tails short because it's my belief that the tailing represents the anal vent of a minnow. A two-inch-long minnow doesn't have a very big anal vent! Taper the abrupt end of the yarn segment with a snip off the top and another off the bottom.

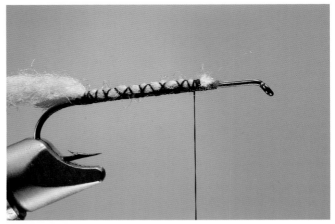

3. There are two methods of tying on a strand of yarn for a streamer body. One way is to tie the yarn to the hook beginning about a hook-gap space behind the hook eye and lashing it down all the way to the tailing, then winding it forward to the starting point.

4. Yarn body with no taper at tail: This method creates a minor problem with the first turn at the tailing. It's difficult to create a slightly tapered body at the first couple of turns.

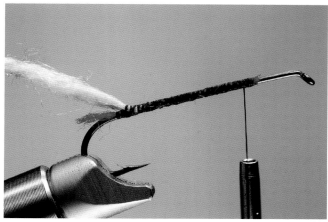

5. A variation to this method is to use only a single strand of yarn. Tie it down as described above, and wind it forward to one hook-gap space behind the eye, then back to the rear and forward again. It's a simple matter if you have a rotary vise. You can create a tapered rear to the body by returning forward a turn or two before you get to the very end of the shank. The end result is three layers of a single strand of yarn.

7. Twist the tapered end of the yarn and tie it to the hook about a hook-eye space from the end of the shank. Then twist the yarn two or three more times and wind it forward in tightly nesting turns. You can add to the taper by allowing the yarn to untwist slightly once you have begun. This will allow you to overlap one or two of the strands to create a very smooth body all the way to the tie-down spot just behind the hook eye.

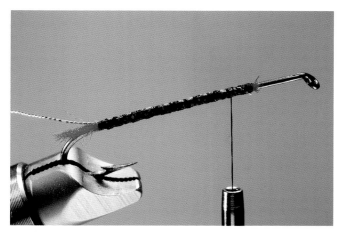

6. My preferred method of using four-strand yarn on a streamer body is to first pull some fibers from the end of the yarn with my thumbnail and forefinger to make the end of the yarn segment much thinner and tapered.

8. If your streamer pattern calls for ribbing of any kind, you should attach it to the hook about a hook-gap space behind the eye, and lash it down all the way to the end of the shank before you tie on any kind of body material. Whether you reverse-wind the ribbing or wrap it in the same direction is not a crucial matter. Reverse-wrapping the ribbing does make the body of the fly more durable.

Some of the older streamer patterns, such as the Black-Nose Dace and the Mickey Finn, call for a flat tinsel body ribbed with oval tinsel. It's OK to know how to do this, but those patterns were devised before the invention of braided Mylar tinsel. I am of the opinion (and I have a few!) that the oval tinsel ribbing was to add a little flash and durability to the body of these flies, because if a trout's tooth cut the tinsel body, it would come apart.

Now we have Mylar braided tinsel, which is available in a variety of diameters and allows us to tie durable streamer bodies with plenty of flash. If a trout's tooth snags the braid and leaves a couple of loose ends flailing about, you can merely snip them off and have a clean-looking body again.

Braided Mylar tinsel

There are two methods to attach this material to the hook to create a smooth body. One is to tie it down about a hook-gap space behind the hook eye, lash it down all the way to the end of the shank, bring the thread back forward, and then wind it forward in tightly nesting wraps. This will create a very slim body profile, which I like in most of my streamers. You can also use this method when tying small wet flies if you use the smallest-diameter braided Mylar available.

Single layer braided Mylar streamer body

A second way of attaching braided Mylar tinsel to the hook is to first fray the end bit, and then tie it down just in front of the tailing tie-down. *Note:* If you have used

lead substitute wire to weight your fly, tie in the end of the braided Mylar just behind the rear wrap of wire, lash it down to the tailing, and wind it forward. It's a simple matter to manipulate the braided Mylar to overlap itself to create a taper that will hide the lead wraps.

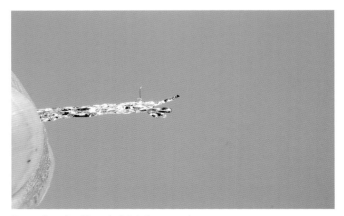

Frayed end of braided Mylar tinsel

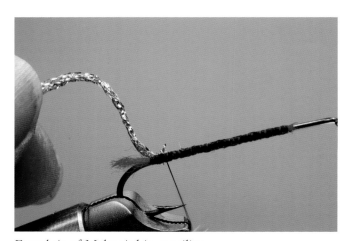

Frayed tip of Mylar tied in at tailing

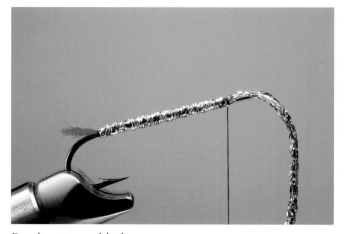

Resultant tapered body

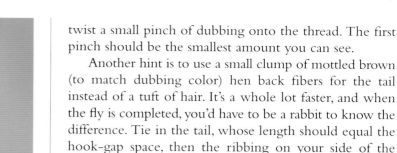

Braided Mylar tied in just behind lead wire

Completed braided Mylar body over lead wraps

It's fairly easy to eliminate bumps in the dubbed bodies of nymphs. All you have to do is make certain that the dubbing you apply to the thread is absolutely smooth and slightly tapered. If there is a bump or thin spot in the dubbing rope, you will have to exercise a little extra care that the blemish doesn't transfer to the body of the nymph. It can be a problem when tying Gold-Ribbed Hare's Ear Nymphs, because hare's ear dubbing is quite coarse. The best way to eliminate thin spots and bulges in the dubbing thread is to apply the dubbing in small pinches and overlap each tiny pinch to create a smooth taper to the rope.

I buy hare's masks by the dozen and match them for slight color variations according to the flies I'm going to tie. And I use all the hair on the mask, including the coarse little fibers on the ears. Clip all the hair off, put it in a pile on your bench, mix it by hand as best you can, and then blend it in a coffee grinder. The finer hairs around the cheeks of the mask will help hold the coarser hairs together when you take a pinch to twist onto the thread. I wouldn't recommend applying dubbing wax to the tying thread, since this makes it very difficult to prevent lumps in the dubbing rope. I find it much more effective to stroke my forefinger on the wax, and then

twist a small pinch of dubbing onto the thread. The first pinch should be the smallest amount you can see.

Another hint is to use a small clump of mottled brown (to match dubbing color) hen back fibers for the tail instead of a tuft of hair. It's a whole lot faster, and when the fly is completed, you'd have to be a rabbit to know the difference. Tie in the tail, whose length should equal the hook-gap space, then the ribbing on your side of the hook. The reason for this is that you should reverse-wind the ribbing. Tying it in on your side of the hook will set it up to come up around on the top of the body on the first turn. Bring the thread back to the end of the hook shank and begin applying dubbing.

Hare's ear tail and ribbing tied on

Dubbing rope ready to wind

A common fault when tying nymphs is to stop the abdomen too soon. Then the tier usually ties in the wing-pad material and dubs the thorax area. It always results in a thin spot in the body and a skinny little wing pad, because there is nothing under it to keep it wide and flat.

Completed Hare's Ear Nymph with skinny wing pad

Completed Gold-Ribbed Hare's Ear Nymph

Solve the problem by carrying the abdomen dubbing into the thorax area, wind the gold wire forward, tie it off and trim, and then apply the wing-pad material about a hook-gap space behind the eye. By the way, for your gold wire, get brass beading wire from a craft store, which is usually sold in two or three different gauges, or diameters. It's a lot better material than the brittle stuff sold in fly shops and doesn't seem to corrode or turn color with age. I use dark gray goose quill segments for the wing pad. Liberally spray the entire quill with Krylon Workable Fixatif before separating the segments. I like to tie the segments in with the wide part (that portion that was closest to the center quill) down and the shiny side up. If you need a black wing pad, simply color the goose segment with a black permanent marker.

Wing-pad material tied on

Then dub a rather loose and fatter thorax area, pull the quill segment forward, tie it down, and clip off the excess. Use a dubbing teaser to brush out the appearance of legs on the bottom of the thorax.

Apply all the techniques described above to the tying of any ribbed, dubbed body nymph with a wing pad.

Quill Segment Techniques

Speaking of quill segment wing pads on nymphs, I tie a few nymphs with a quill segment tied on as a shellback for the entire length of the body. Oftentimes when this is done, a small wrinkle appears at the tie-down point just in front of the tailing material. This little wrinkle can be avoided very easily, and it begins with selecting the width of the segment. The tip of the segment should be trimmed off at a point where the clipped-off tip is about as wide as two hook-eye spaces. Tie the clipped tip on top of the hook, with the dull side down, immediately in front of the last turn of thread on the tailing. To do this without getting a wrinkle in the tie-down area, try the following:

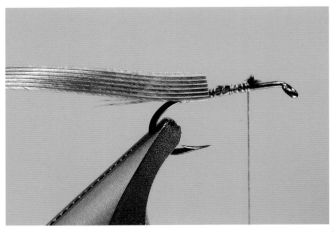

1. Place the tip of the segment slightly on your side of the hook, with about half a hook-gap space left for the tie-down.

2. Shorten the thread between the bobbin tube and the hook shank to about ¼ inch and begin to take one loose turn over the quill segment tip. There can be no tension on the thread, because that's what makes the wrinkle.

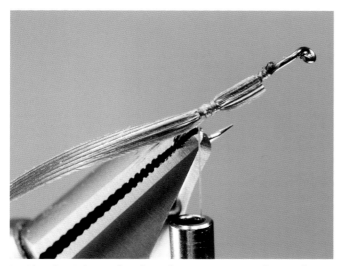

3. Slowly tighten the thread to encompass the quill segment tip. The result should be a quill segment tip that is nicely curved around to each side of the hook at the tie-in point.

Pheasant Tail Nymph

I've never been able to tie a Pheasant Tail Nymph successfully using only one clump of pheasant tail fibers. I always seem to end up with a lump at the very first turn of fibers just in front of the tail. Another frustration is that a single clump of pheasant tail fibers often isn't long enough to serve as both tailing and body material. I solve these problems by selecting a pheasant tail feather that has fibers too short for anything but tailing and use it for tailing only. Then I select another tail feather that has quite long fibers to use for the body material. Here's how to tie a smooth-bodied Pheasant Tail Nymph:

1. Attach black 6/0 thread to the hook about a hook-gap space behind the eye, wind to the end of the shank, and clip off the tag.

2. Select three short fibers for the tail. Stroke the fibers so that they are perpendicular to the quill. This will even the tips. Clip rather than pull them off.

3. Tie the tailing fibers to the hook at the end of the shank to extend beyond the shank by one hook-gap distance. Then tie brass wire to your side of the hook. This will set up the wire for a reverse wrap that will not cut any body fibers as you spiral-wind it forward.

4. Pick up the pheasant tail feather with long fibers, stroke the fibers to stand perpendicular to the quill to even the tips, and clip off a segment that is about as wide as the hook-gap distance.

5. Clip off about ¹⁄4 inch of the tips and tie the remainder to the top of the hook.

6. Wind the fibers forward, allowing some fibers to overlap previous turns to create a slight body taper, to a point that is about half a hook-gap space behind the eye. Tie them down and clip off the butts.

7. Carefully reverse-wind the brass wire over the body, leaving about a hook-eye space between each turn of wire. Tie down the wire just in front of the body material with three or four firm turns of thread, and clip off the remaining wire tag. Bring the thread back to hang at a point that is one full hook-gap space behind the eye. Then the body is ribbed and the thread is ready for the wing pad.

The Pheasant Tail Nymph wing pad is supposed to be a segment of black wing quill. The best material I have found for this is dyed black wild turkey tail segments. When tied in with the shiny side down and pulled forward over the thorax area, the turkey segment offers a glistening wing pad. Natural shine!

8. Tie the black turkey segment on top of the shoulder of the body at its widest point and with the shiny side down, tip to the rear, one hook-gap space behind the eye.

Note: The original recipe for this fly requires a continuation of pheasant tail fibers for the thorax area. I've never liked the look of it. Not buggy enough to suit me. Some tiers use peacock herl for the thorax, but again, it doesn't look buggy enough to me. So I use hare's ear nymph dubbing and tease it out after winding it on the hook.

9. Bring the tying thread forward to hang one hook-eye space behind the eye, and apply hare's ear dubbing to the thread, creating a tapered and rather loose dubbing rope.

10. Wind the dubbing to the rear, creating a thorax that will be at least twice the diameter of the shoulder of the body. Bring the thread forward over the top of the thorax to flatten it, and allow it to hang just behind the eye.

11. Pull the turkey segment forward, take a couple turns of thread over it just behind the eye, and clip off the excess. Whip-finish, tease out the thorax a bit with a dubbing teaser, and apply a small drop of lacquer to the thread head and a liberal amount over the black wing pad. There is your completed Pheasant Tail Nymph.

Eliminating bumps in floss-bodied nymph and wet flies is easy to do as long as you use single-strand floss. If you can't find single-strand floss in your local fly shop, go first to a fabric shop and purchase a small container of sewing machine bobbins. Then carefully unwind a spool of four-strand floss, and wind the single strands onto the sewing machine bobbins. These bobbins fit nicely in a Matarelli type midge bobbin. I have found that one of the best ways to prevent fraying of the floss during this process is to string the four-strand floss around your room, over the wood arms of chairs and anything else that has a smooth surface. Use a spring-loaded clothespin to clip the ends to something heavy, such as a book cover. Winding the floss onto the bobbins is easy if you use a variable-speed drill and something like a pencil or pen that you can fit into both the drill chuck and the hole in the bobbin. When you get near the end of one strand of floss, knot another strand to it and continue winding. If you don't have a variable-speed drill, wear rubber gloves and wind it on by hand. This will take a little while.

Put the hook in your vise and attach tying thread that is the same color as the floss, one shade lighter, or white (dark thread will show through the floss) about one hook-eye space behind the eye, with only five or six turns of thread. Attach the very tip of the floss at the thread starting point.

Thread and floss attached behind the hook eye

Wind the single-strand floss to near the end of the shank in carefully nested turns. Stop winding to the rear about half a hook-eye space before the end of the shank. This will allow you to begin winding it forward without an obvious fold in the floss and create the slightest body taper.

Floss wound to the rear

Wind the floss forward to the starting point. When you arrive at the thread tie-down point, unwind the thread that is holding the tip of the floss, take one turn of floss over the tip, and tie it down with two or three turns of thread. This will avoid any kind of bump in the thorax area.

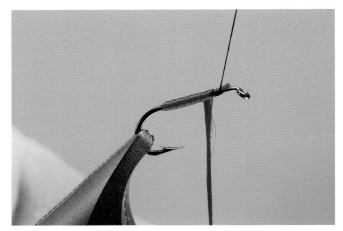

Unwinding tying thread

Winding floss over tie-down area

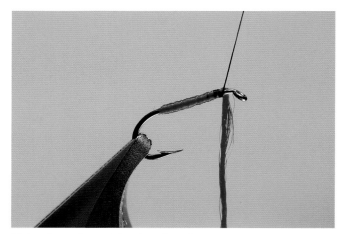

Tying down floss with tying thread

Lift the remaining floss, and place your scissor tips parallel to the shank and over the hook eye to clip off the floss coming from the bobbin. Take one or two more turns of thread, and then apply the soft-hackle collar if that's what comes next.

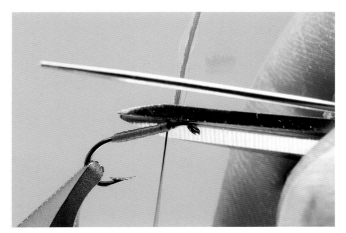

Snipping off floss

Floss-bodied fly patterns often require some kind of ribbing to provide a little sparkle and reinforce this very fragile body material that will get snagged by trout teeth quite easily. Use the finest wire you can find for the ribbing. Tie it to the hook just behind the eye, as described above for tying on the floss. Then lash the wire all the way to the end of the shank, but keep it on your side of the hook shank. This will hide the first turn of reverse-wrapped wire under the body as you wind it forward over the floss. Untie the thread that is holding the last turn of floss to tie down the wire, and clip off the wire, as described above for trimming floss.

Wire lashed to hook

Wire reverse-wrapped

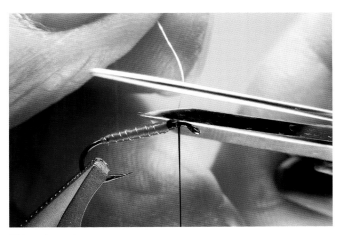

Trimming wire

Preventing bumps in the bodies of dubbed dry flies is easy to do as long as you start applying the dubbing to the thread correctly. There also are a couple of important characteristics of the bodies of the adult natural mayfly, caddisfly, and stonefly to keep in mind. For one, none of them have fuzzy bodies. These are adult aquatic insects, and if their bodies were fuzzy, they'd stick to the water. Instead, their bodies are completely opaque, waxy, and smooth in appearance, designed by nature to repel water. Yet we see dubbing material on the market that is so stiff, it's next to impossible to dub a smooth body on any adult fly imitation. Manufacturers of dubbing material sometimes advertise its translucency as a positive feature. Yet the bodies of the adult flies are not translucent. Look up the word in a dictionary. *Translucent* means "light passing through." I think a lot of people confuse light *reflection* with translucency. Light does reflect off the shiny, waxy bodies of these insects.

So to avoid having bumpy, fuzzy bodies on your flies when you use dubbing, always try to find the finest-fibered dubbing you can. (See chapter 6 for an in-depth discussion.)

Attach tying thread that is the same color as the dubbing you will use, or one shade lighter, and tie the tailing material to the hook. Then bring the tying thread back to the beginning of the hook bend in preparation for applying dubbing to the thread. Stroke the pad of your forefinger on some dubbing wax and rub it against your thumb pad. If you can feel a bit of tackiness, you got it right. Take the tiniest pinch of dubbing you can see, and apply it to the thread very firmly by twisting it in only one direction. Think of impregnating the thread with dubbing as you do this. The amount of dubbing on the thread at this point should increase its diameter by only one thread width. Squeeze the dubbing onto the thread with enough pressure between your thumb and forefinger that the tips of both turn white. It's the only way to achieve a smooth body with dubbing. Keep adding small pinches of dubbing to very gradually increase the diameter of the slightly tapered dubbing rope.

First pinch of dubbing applied

Second and third pinches added

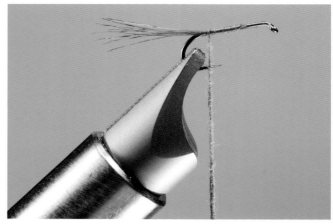

Completed smooth dubbing rope, which is very slim and only slightly tapered.

Carefully wind the dubbing rope forward to create a carrot-shaped body on your fly. It is at this point that you will discover the value of having created a very thin and slightly tapered dubbing rope. If a small void in the dubbed body appears, you can go back over the spot with another turn of dubbing. If a lump appears, you can unwind a turn of dubbing and squeeze it by twisting very firmly, then carefully rewind it to check the result.

Completed slim, slightly tapered, and smooth dry-fly body with no fuzz

Some dry flies require ribbing of either fine gold or silver wire or single-strand floss. Start the thread on the hook as described for tying the tailing onto a dry fly, and tie on the tailing fibers. Bring the thread back to the starting point, and attach the ribbing tip directly on top of the thread starting point. Lash it to the rear on your side of the hook, stopping one thread width beyond the last turn of thread over the tailing material. This will allow you to make one reverse wrap of wire or floss without disturbing the body material.

Tailing and fine wire tied on

Construct the body, reverse-wind the ribbing forward over the shoulder, and tie it off in front of the shoulder. Snip off the excess and continue tying your fly.

Completed wire-ribbed body

I've written about quill-bodied flies many times, and I've been teaching classes for almost twenty years on the use of stripped and dyed rooster hackle quills for body material on mayfly patterns and how to tie them. One of the exciting things about tying flies for a living is that I am always discovering some little nuance to handling materials or thread, thus eliminating the problem or two that occasionally crop up. One of these problems is how to always be certain that the quills are in the proper position when tying a fly that requires two quills for the body, such as a size 16 and larger fly. If the two quills are not precisely aligned, they will wind on the hook side by side.

Using a size 16 and larger hook requires two quills simply to achieve the correct body taper. One quill will make a body that is too thin; the answer to that failing is to use two quills. One quill must be twice the diameter of the other when laid side by side. The thinner quill becomes an underbody, which the thicker quill covers as you wind them both forward at the same time.

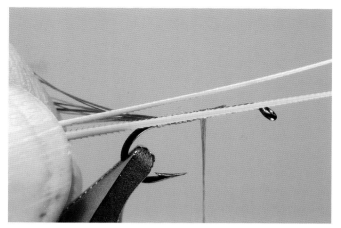

Two quills

Clip off the tips of both quills at a point where the thicker one is about the same diameter as the hook eye. This will automatically provide a segmentation effect to match that of the natural insect.

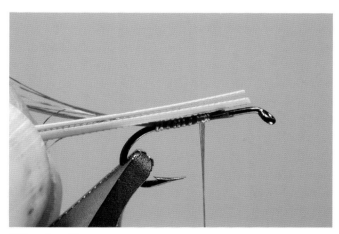

Clipped quills

Now here comes the little nuance I discovered. Tie the clipped tips, with butts to the rear, to the top of the hook, one hook gap behind the eye. Then lash them to the rear with tying thread *while holding the quill butts and angling them slightly toward your side of the hook.* This will ensure that the thinner quill stays in touch with the thicker one as you wrap thread over both. If you hold them straight back over the hook, thread torque will move the thinner one, creating a tiny space between them. Then when you start to wrap them forward, they will go on the hook side by side, which is not what you want.

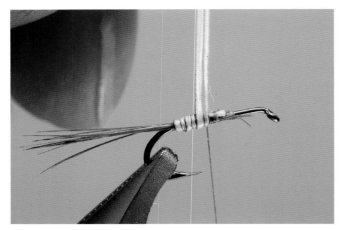

Winding quills forward

Quills side by side (no body taper)

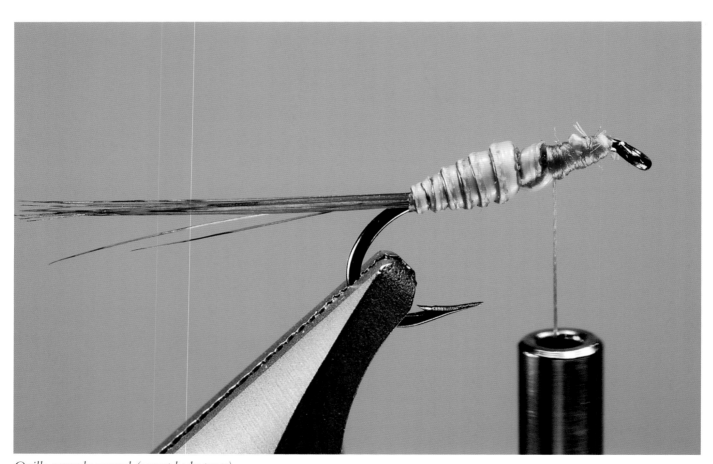

Quills properly wound (correct body taper)

CHAPTER 4

Avoiding Trapped Hackles

Hackling seems to generate the most discussion about how to correctly tie dry-fly dun patterns. One school of thought says there is only one correct way to tie the hackle to the hook, place to tie it, and technique to wrap it. Another group maintains that it doesn't matter how it's tied to the hook, where it's attached, or how it's wrapped, as long as you achieve the desired effect. If the dry fly floats the way you want it and fools fish, who's to say you didn't do it right? And then there is the tier or fly salesman's trick of tossing the fly onto a tabletop to show you how it bounces as he exclaims about the fine stiff hackle he uses on all his flies. That would be great if trout ate flies from the top of your table. I've never seen a dry fly bounce off the water the way it does from my table. The bouncing fly is supposed to indicate that it was hackled with the finest and stiffest hackle available and will float on the water on its hackle tips. It never happens! Next time you go fishing, cast your fly about fifteen feet upstream and allow it to float down right in front of you. Bend over and look at it carefully. I'll bet you a six-pack that you'll find that the fly is floating flush in the surface and not on its tippy toes. It's not the vertical hackle fibers that float your fly, it's the horizontal ones.

The cocked-down tail and extremely stiff dry-fly hackle technique evolved during the days when it was desirable to keep your fly from getting wet and the most popular dry-fly treatment was a paraffin and white gas treatment. Tiers and fly fishers shaved some paraffin into a container of white gas, shook it up vigorously to dissolve the paraffin, and then dipped their dry flies into it. The evaporating white gas left a microscopic layer of paraffin on the fly, which prevented water from entering the materials. It worked for a short time, and then you had to change flies. This is among the reasons why we still carry half a dozen flies of the same size and pattern.

Many of the so-called rules of hackling have been changed by the development of today's genetically engineered hackles. The dry-fly neck and saddle feathers available to us these days have longer, thinner quills with a hackle density and stiffness we only dreamed about just ten years ago. Things are to the point these days that you almost have to work at it to tie a poorly hackled dry fly. That is, until you tie off the hackle tip after the last wrap of hackle. This is usually where things go horribly wrong.

Most fly-tying instruction books and magazine articles have very clear instructions on how the hackle should be prepared for tying to the hook, how to place it on the hook, exactly where it should be held prior to tying down, how to tie it down, and how to wind it around the hook. They then tell you to tie off the hackle tip on top of the hook, clip it away, and whip-finish. Much of this information repeats what has been written for the last hundred years and does not take into account today's genetic improvements of the neck and saddle hackle feathers.

As a matter of fact, there are few specific instructions on how to prevent trapping hackle fibers when you bring the thread over the hackle tip prior to tying down, clipping off the tip, and whip-finishing. The following series of photos illustrates what has been the way we're supposed to do it.

Resultant trapped hackle over hook eye

Some tiers have written that we should use some sort of hackle guard or fold the hackles back with the thumb and forefinger to avoid the problem of trapping them over the hook eye, but this creates the problem of trapping them in the other direction. In other words, they are forced back into the hackle collar, as shown in the next photo.

Hackle fibers trapped back into hackle collar

Dry-fly dun with hackle tip straight up over eye and thread going over top

New materials always require learning how we must handle them to make them look right after they're tied on the hook, so that we achieve the desired effect when they're completed. The new high-density fibered hackles are an excellent example of a material for which we need to learn some new techniques.

Prepare the hackle butt by snipping away enough barbs so that when you begin to wind it around the hook, there is a little bare quill at the beginning of the first turn. This will prevent the appearance of trapped hackle fibers as you begin winding it. Place the butt on the hook with the shiny side up, tie it down with three or four turns of thread, and bring the thread forward to hang at a point that will be the *exact rear of the head.* I prefer to tie the butt of the hackle in front of the wings, which will help make the diameter here closer to that behind the wings. This is an excellent way to prevent a cone-shaped hackle collar.

Prepared hackle butt showing bare quill

Wind the hackle collar by lifting the hackle up and making the first turn with it go down in front of the far wing and up behind both wings. Make two or three turns behind the wing, bring the hackle forward under both wings, and wind forward. When you get to the last turn of hackle, instead of bringing the tip up to the top of the hook and holding it there while you bring the thread up and over it, as shown on page 38, bring the hackle tip around and stop winding when it's level with the floor, with the hackle tip pointing straight toward your stomach, as shown in the next photo.

Hackle tip in horizontal position

Hold the hackle tip in this position while you reach around with your materials hand and grasp the bobbin to come around and *behind* the hackle tip. (*Note:* If the thread is hanging down immediately behind the hook eye, it will slide hackle fibers forward and trap them as you wind the thread over the tip. The tying thread must be left hanging at the rear of the head space.) When the tying thread is level with the hackle tip, wind them both up toward the top of the hook and down to floor level on the far side at the same time. Stop the hackle tip when it's at floor level, and continue with the tying thread to complete one full turn of thread over the tip. Take one more turn of thread, then pull the hackle tip back up to the top as you continue to make one more complete turn of thread. Clip off the hackle tip by pointing the scissor tips straight toward the fly, as shown in the photo below.

Hackle tip and thread on the far side level with the floor

Hackle tip straight up with two turns of thread and no trapped hackle

Cutting off hackle tip

Winding both the hackle tip and the thread in this fashion allows the tying thread to slide through the hackle fibers at a slight angle rather than over the top of them, trapping few if any fibers over the hook eye.

Completed fly

With today's neck hackle, trapping hackle fibers doesn't seem to be quite as problematic as with the new high-grade saddle hackles, but it's more of a problem than it used to be. The feathers from both the neck and the saddle patch have many more hackle fibers per inch than they did just a few years ago, but saddle hackles seem far more densely fibered than neck hackles. The favored method of tying on the hackle butt has been with the dull side up or forward, which causes the fibers to lean forward slightly. It is believed this will help support the fly a little better, but it also increases the chances for more hackle fibers to be trapped over the eye when tying off the tip. The risk of trapped fibers over the hook eye when using saddle hackle (with the dull side up) is greatly increased when the hackles are cupped, with the fibers all curved slightly toward the center quill. If you tie on a cupped hackle feather with the dull side forward, it's almost impossible to tie it off without trapping a bunch of hackles. By the way, even if you trim off all the trapped hackles before whip-finishing, the fly head will probably come apart, since the hackle fibers are very slick and will easily slide out from under the head.

The hackle fibers from today's genetic birds are so stiff that it hardly matters which side of the feather faces forward. In fact, in order to further reduce the possibility of trapped fibers over the hook eye, I currently tie in the hackle butt with the shiny side up or forward. This makes the shiny side of the hackle fibers face forward and appear to be more perpendicular to the hook as the feather is wound forward.

If the above seems like somewhat of a departure from traditional methods, consider the parachute hackle collar. I can think of about half a dozen methods that all are supposed to be the easiest and best way to tie the hackle stem to the fly, wrap it, and tie it off. I've tried all of them and always end up with more trapped hackles than I'd like to see or find the procedure very awkward to do. It doesn't really matter which method is used to tie the feather on or how it is wound, as long as the completed horizontal collar doesn't come loose during use or have a bunch of trapped hackles either up or down on the post. I am convinced that the absolute best hackle to use on a parachute collar is the most expensive saddle hackle you can find. It will have a tremendous barb count per inch of feather; very stiff hackle fibers, which means that it will take fewer turns of hackle to complete a good-looking horizontal collar that will support the fly on the surface film; and usually no web.

My favorite method of attaching the hackle to a parachute pattern is to tie the trimmed quill to the side of the hook facing me at a 45-degree angle above the hook shank with the tip toward the rear, as shown in the photo below. Notice that the shiny side of the feather is up and the fibers are horizontal. It is also important that the hackle feather be trimmed a little farther back on the side that will go around the post first. This will prevent any fibers from becoming pinched up or down on the first turn.

Parachute hackle stem tied to hook

The first turn of hackle will be the top turn, and each succeeding turn will be directly below the previous one. This method absolutely prevents the hackle collar from sliding up the post and coming off, since each turn is pulling down on its predecessor.

Parachute Hackle Technique

Tying off the tip on a parachute hackled fly has always presented problems with trapped hackle fibers. It is especially true with today's genetic hackles. I prefer to use high-grade saddle hackle on my parachute patterns because of the finer quill and improved hackle fiber count, but the extra hackle count also increases the probability that more fibers will be trapped when I tie off the tip. There is a way to prevent all but one or two hackle fibers from being trapped. In fact, often times you'll be able to tie off the hackle with no trapped hackle fibers whatsoever! Try the following:

1. On the last or bottom turn of hackle around the post, angle it down on the far side of the hook to come around under all previous turns of hackle. This will capture any fibers that are hanging down and return them to a horizontal position. Then bring the hackle back up to clear the hook eye, and continue wrapping until the hackle stem is parallel to the hook shank, as shown in the photo above.

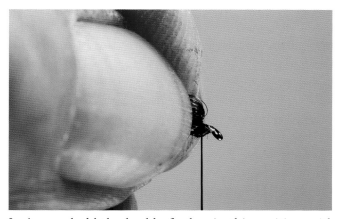

2. As you hold the hackle feather in this position with your right hand, reach over with your materials hand to stroke all the fibers in the collar slightly up and back toward the bend of the hook, as shown in the above photo. Your bobbin hand is now holding the hackle feather tightly to the side of the hook in its rearward position.

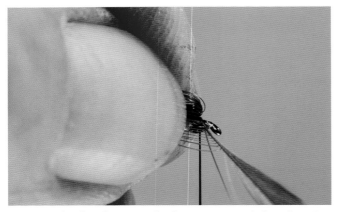

3. Keep the forefinger pad of your materials hand against the head space, and use your other hand to gently pull the hackle feather from your materials hand grasp to a position slightly forward of the hook eye. You may see several hackle fiber tips still trapped in your materials hand grip, as shown in the above photo.

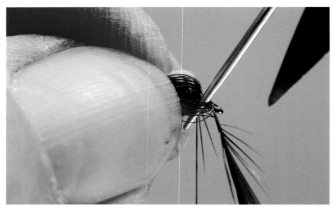

4. Simply use your bodkin to stroke the hackle fibers out, as demonstrated above.

5. Take two turns of thread over the V created by those hackle fibers you're still holding fast and those you just released, as shown in the above photo.

6. Gently pull on the hackle to completely tighten the collar, take a couple more turns of thread to anchor, lift the tip, clip it off by aiming the scissors directly at the front of the fly, and whip-finish by stroking the hackle collar to the rear once again.

7. Completed parachute hackle collar: Some of the hackle fibers may appear to be displaced by all the stroking you have just done. Not to fear! Simply stroke them back into their original position with your thumb and forefinger. Apply a drop of head lacquer to the top of the hackle collar and another to the bottom of the head.

I don't worry very much about a couple of unruly hackle fibers in the flies I tie unless they are going into someone's collection. Most of the time, it's wind, bind, snip, and whip. In fact, hackling flies is much like some other operations in fly tying, in that the slower you go, the more problems you are apt to create. As a rule, go about it as if you really know what you're doing, even if you don't! Nine times out of ten, it'll come out OK. If you find a trapped hackle or two, snip them off or pluck them out with a pair of tweezers. It's what the professionals do.

CHAPTER 5

Crisper Hair Wings and Tails

This chapter has some hints for those of you who tie flies for collections, magazine article photographs, or to impress your friends. I've done a lot of all the above in the last thirty years and have learned a couple of things I'd like to pass on to you. Some of you already know them, because I have seen your flies and they are crisp indeed.

I'm not going into hackle selection here, but the deer or elk body hair that you choose when tying flies with hair wings or tails. The best hair for tailing on large drakes, such as Green and Brown Drakes, is found on the back of the elk just in front of the blond rump patch. There is a band of hair about 4 or 5 inches wide that goes about one-third of the way down each hip and across the center of the back. This hair is 3 to 4 inches long, very straight, and buoyant, but it's not quite as hollow as flank hair, so it doesn't flare as much when tied onto the hook. These qualities make it the perfect hair for tailing and Wulff-style hair wings. You can make it flare if you really bear down and create a lot of thread tension. But even then, it doesn't flare as much as flank hair. Flank hair is good for spinning bass bug bodies and muddler or hopper heads, because it is of a larger diameter and has more air space within each hair. You can make flank hair work for the wing on caddis patterns with a little care in how much thread tension you exert and where you make the first few turns of anchoring thread.

I'll deal with hair tails first. You will notice that not all the hairs on the patch that I recommend above are the same length.

Bent hair patch showing uneven hair lengths

If you clip off a small clump of hair, remove all the underfur, and stack it in a hair stacker, it will look as in the following photo.

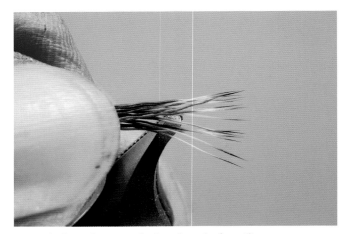

Raggedy hair clump stacked and ready for tailing

This is a neat tail clump, but it's not really crisp. That's because the shorter hairs in the clump also have shorter blond bands and black tips than the longer hairs. The very long hairs in the above photo have much longer blond bands and longer black tips. The difference in the length of blond bands and black tips is what makes the hair clump appear to be a bit ragged, even though the tips are all even.

To solve this problem, clip off a small clump of hair, pull out all the longest hairs, and remove the underfur. Then hold the remaining clump by its tips between the thumb and forefinger of your materials hand, and flick out the shorter hairs with the forefinger of your other hand.

Pulling out the longest hairs

Removing underfur

Flicking out shorter hairs

Now put the remaining clump of hair in your stacker, give it a couple of taps, and notice the difference. It's a minor thing that I'm positive the trout couldn't care less about, but if you want to improve the appearance of the hair tails on your flies, this is a good thing to do.

Neat hair clump for Wulff wing

Crisp hair clump after cleaning and stacking

Tying on hair clump

Crisp hair tail

The amount of hair you use for tailing is a matter of personal choice, governed to a degree by hook size and type of fly. It's easy to use too much!

If you want to tie some Wulff-type hair-wing flies, use the hair from the same area of the elk, and prepare it as described above. For the wings, use a little more than double the amount that you used for the tail. Again, it's a matter of personal choice. But be careful with hair wings. If you use too much hair in the wing, the fly will be top-heavy and roll to one side on the water. The arm of each side of the V-shaped wing must be an equal distance from absolute vertical. Be extremely careful about the shape of the V and its placement.

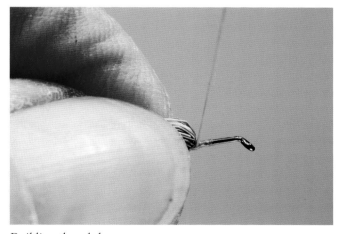

Building thread dam

Fanning hair clump with thumbnail

Dividing wing

Figure-eight thread wraps

Posting each wing with thread

Tying wings on elk-hair caddis patterns and other down-wing patterns can be a little frustrating. Again, your choice of hair and where on the hide it comes from will make a major difference in how much trouble you have creating a wing to your liking. Elk flank hair seems to be the material of choice, although white-tailed deer body hair works just as well. The individual hairs from a white-tailed deer flank are noticeably smaller in diameter than those from an elk flank, which makes deer flank hair a good choice for small hook sizes. The colors and markings, however, are nearly identical. Hairs from elk are widely used in the West, where they are prevalent, and those from white-tailed deer are widely used in the Midwest and East, because that's where they live. We all use what is easily available.

Elk flank hair and white-tailed deer flank hair

You will still need to stack the flank hair from both the deer and elk, but there isn't such a noticeable difference between long and short hairs from either animal, unless it was taken from down near the belly. Sometimes you get lucky and find a patch of flank hair that contains hairs that are nearly identical in length. Buy a bunch of it when you can find it! It pays to go to some of the fly-fishing shows in your area not only to meet and greet, but also to look for tying materials. Many of the shops that are exhibiting at these shows bring a lot of fly-tying materials and offer some good prices on them. It gives you a chance to look at other shops' goods and do a little high grading.

To control the amount of flare when tying Elk Hair Caddis or any other hair down-wing pattern, just follow a few simple rules and you'll have great success.

Rule number one: Always taper the front portion of the body right down to the hook-shank diameter. This will prevent excess flaring when you tie in the hair wing. If you are using dyed rooster neck hackle quills for the body, you need to wind the quill forward well into the thorax area, stopping one hook-eye space behind the eye, and attach the hair wing on top of the quill underbody. It's a lot easier to dub the bodies on caddis patterns.

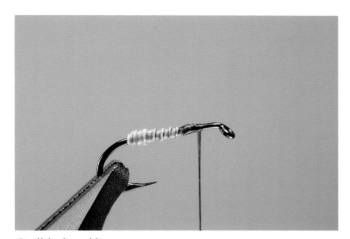

Quill body caddis

Tapered shoulder, dubbed body

Rule number two: Always make a thread base where you intend to tie down the hair clump on a dubbed body.

Thread base

Rule number three: Always take the first few firm anchoring turns of thread in the middle of the area of tie-down. Then wind the thread to the rear with less tension (to control the amount of flare), and wind it forward again to stop one hook-eye space behind the eye. Lift the butts and clip them at an angle. Be careful to distribute the hair evenly around to each side of the hook. This will help keep the fly upright and support it on the surface.

Hair wing tied on

Rule number four: Always leave a hair underbody to wind the hackle on. If you don't do this, you'll end up with a cone-shaped hackle collar.

Hair underbody for hackle winding

Rule number five: Always cut off the hair butts at a shallow angle to allow for a neat head finish.

Hair butts clipped at shallow *angle*

Rule number six: Always clip off the top hackle fibers when tying a hair wing over a palmer-hackled body.

Top hackle fibers clipped off on palmered body

And use less hair! Most tiers use enough hair in the wings on their caddis patterns to tie two or three flies. Take a look at your fly from above after you have tied the wing on. You should be able to see the body through the hair wing. Most caddisfly naturals flutter their wings when they're on the water as they attempt to escape. None of the hair in the top of the wing adds to the buoyancy of the fly. It's the hair on the sides of the wing and the stiff hackle collar that support the fly. Using too much hair is one of the main reasons why tiers have a problem anchoring the wings tightly.

I've yet to see a tent-wing caddis *on* the water! Such flies are the result of tiers looking at photos of insects out of their natural environment and thinking that's how they look on the water. Photographers take pictures of natural caddises when they're resting on a leaf, branch, or rock. Then we use these photos to tie our flies to look the way the naturals do *off* the water. That would be fine if trout ate caddisflies from rocks, leaves, and branches. Have you ever seen a photo of a live fluttering caddis *on the water?*

CHAPTER 6

Dubbing Fine Bodies

No adult aquatic insect has a fuzzy body. That observation is what drove me to tie all my own dry mayfly imitations with stripped and dyed rooster neck hackle quills or wild turkey biots. Both materials are easily dyed to any color you may desire. Not everyone agrees with my preference for body material; some tiers still choose to use a dubbing product. And that's fine. Dubbing is the traditional way to create the body on many mayfly patterns. It takes a little longer to create a finely tapered body without a fuzzy appearance with dubbing, especially with some of the synthetic products available today, because the fibers can be quite spongy.

Synthetic dubbing has been around for several decades and has been highly touted as providing translucence to the completed fly. If you look up the definition of translucent in your dictionary, you will find that it means "letting light pass through." Well, light does not pass through the body of the adult mayfly or caddis or stonefly (except for the spent or spinner stage of some mayflies). Rather, light is reflected from the body of the insect. Hence my preference for quill or biot bodies, since both materials have a waxy appearance and reflect light, and also provide prominent segmentation, much like the natural insect's body.

Three of the finest natural fibers you can use for dubbing the bodies of mayflies are rabbit belly underfur, beaver underfur, or dyed raw silk. Rabbit pelts, in both dyed and natural colors, and beaver dubbing are readily available from most well-stocked fly shops. Silk dubbing is marketed by Kreinik. When purchasing prepared rabbit or beaver dubbing, be sure there are no guard hairs in the package for tying dry flies, or you will end up with a fuzzy or even hairy appearing body. Almost all premixed and packaged rabbit fur and beaver dubbing contain guard hairs simply because it takes too much time to pull them out before clipping and blending. You would be wise to purchase complete skins, cut them into one-inch-wide strips, pull the guard hairs from a strip, and clip and mix your own dubbing blends. But be very careful about the rabbit skins you purchase. Some have been given haircuts! That is to say, the longer guard hairs have been carefully mown off to make the skin appear as if has no guard hairs. Carefully examine the pelt by bending it and looking for guard hair stubs. They are easy to see in the light coming through a window.

In order to achieve a smooth body when using dubbing, you must apply very tiny amounts to the thread. To do this, do not stroke the tying thread with dubbing wax. You'll always get way too much wax on the thread, and you won't be able to control how the dubbing goes onto the thread. You'll get far better results if you stroke your forefinger on the wax, rub it against your thumb, and then apply the dubbing. If you can feel the wax, it's enough. If you use too much, you'll darken the dubbing.

You can create tightly dubbed bodies that are very smooth by pressing your forefinger very hard against your thumb in a rolling motion. Try to imagine that you're impregnating the thread with dubbing. Then, as you wind the dubbed thread around the hook shank, you can create a very densely packed body that is finely tapered, smoother, and far more durable. Some tiers simply stroke the moist bottom lip with the forefinger instead of using dubbing wax. I don't advise this if you tie lots of flies. I used to do it, and my lips almost got infected. Think about it: You have no idea what chemicals are in the dubbing, nor do you know where it's been or what part of the animal it came from!

The absolute finest fiber with no guard hairs is silk dubbing. Silk is the finest-fibered natural material known and makes wonderful dubbing on nearly any size fly you may want to tie. In fact, you can spin silk dubbing onto the tying thread so compactly that a segmented effect can be achieved—even on flies as small as size 26! And silk dubbing reflects light.

No matter which dubbing material you choose to use, always apply the tiniest amount with each pinch. A good way to judge what is a tiny pinch is to look at the smallest amount of dubbing you can balance on the end of your forefinger. If it looks as if it's only a dozen fibers, you may have a little too much! You can always add more if you need to, but once you put it on the thread, it's difficult to remove. Remember that the diameter of the very end of the mayfly body where the tail comes out is no larger than the diameter of the hook you're tying on. You probably got the right amount if the thread becomes twice its diameter after the dubbing has been applied. When this doubled diameter is wound around the hook, it will become twice its own diameter. The first pinch of dubbing you apply to the thread should taper down to the same diameter as that of the thread itself. Then keep adding more to build a very narrow taper by applying tiny pinches of dubbing and squeezing it firmly as you roll it around the thread. You know you're using the right amount of pressure between your thumb and forefinger if the pads of both are turning white.

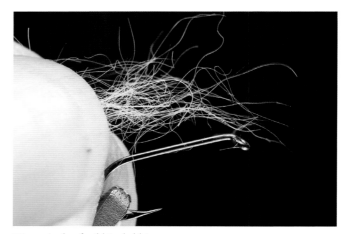

First pinch of rabbit dubbing

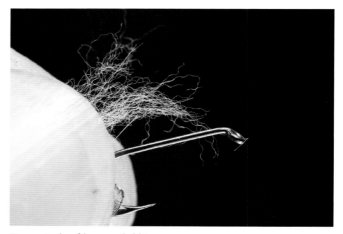

First pinch of beaver dubbing

First pinch of silk dubbing

Silk dubbed body

Rabbit dubbed body

Beaver dubbed body

With the spread of Asian bird flu, we may all have to begin to look back to dubbed or biot bodies on our flies, since I don't think there is going to be a chicken or duck left alive in all of that continent! The disease is close to becoming an international crisis.

Some tiers like to mix some fine synthetic sparkle material into their dubbing blends. Most of these I have seen contain way too much sparkle. The idea is to get the fish's attention, not blind it with the glare. Take a good, close look at the body of the natural you're trying to imitate, and I highly doubt that you'll see any sparkle. Reflection yes, sparkle no. If you still want to add a little sparkle, choose the finest-fibered material you can find, cut it into lengths slightly less than a quarter of an inch, and add just a pinch of it to your dubbing blend. The finest-fibered materials will allow you to create a finely tapered and dense body without much of a fuzzy appearance. Very short silk fibers also work well for this. The best color to choose is pearlescent or natural white silk. Neither will change the basic color of the natural mix much but will add a few sparkles to it.

CHAPTER 7

What Color Is It?

I was fishing the Henry's Fork near Last Chance, Idaho, when I asked another angler what he was catching all his fish on. His answer was a string of Latin names that didn't mean a thing to me. When I asked him what color it was, he looked at me as though I were from a foreign country, then looked at his fly and said, "It's green." I said, "Yeah, but what color of green is it?" "It's kinda olive green." This narrowed it down a little, but I was still at a loss.

It has been documented by a number of fisheries biologists that trout can perceive colors. It's still questionable whether they see them as we do. I maintain that if we can duplicate the colors we see in the naturals into the flies we tie, then maybe the trout will mistake them for naturals. The only way we could be certain about all of this would be to ask a trout what it sees. After more than forty years of trout fishing, I'm convinced that color does make a difference in my success rate.

The problem with any discussion about color is that the actual color of an object we look at, the name we give it, and what that means to someone else can differ. A number of lengthy articles and charts have been published that address colors, but it seems there is always something lacking. Some of this is because the colors are not reproduced accurately in the printing process, but much of it is because of differences in how colors are identified. I think the only way to express the true color of the materials we use to tie flies is to relate them to natural objects that we all have access to every day. Yet this idea must be accurate. I have yet to see a flank feather from a wood duck that is lemon yellow, for example. A brown drake is not brown, and a blue-winged olive doesn't have blue wings. Terms like these can be very confusing to the newcomer to fly tying. When I first began tying, I took the terms literally and tied some weird-looking flies.

I think of lime green or lemon yellow as the color of the rind, not the inside of the fruit. Yet fly-tying materials labeled lime green are often closer to fluorescent yellow-green. And what really is olive green? I think of it as the color of green olives in a jar. But when I go to a fly shop and look at dubbing material or dyed feathers and hair, there are any number of shades of olive: light olive, medium olive, dark olive, olive brown, yellow olive. It seems to be up to the manufacturer of the product what the color shall be called. Not many of them relate to things we all see every day. Adding to this confusion is that medium olive by manufacturer A is a different color than that by manufacturer B, and few of them match the color of the natural insect.

Cinnamon is another. Does this refer to the cinnamon stick or ground cinnamon? Each is a different color. Is chocolate brown the color of milk chocolate or semisweet? And sky blue depends entirely on where you live. The sky is a lot bluer at five thousand feet than it is at sea level. What about dun? It's a gray of some kind. There are sandy dun, smoky dun, light dun, medium dun, and dark dun, just to name a few, and variations to each. Is charcoal gray in this category?

I've been trying to categorize colors according to some sort of standard for a lot of years now, and here is what I came up with:

• Yellow is the color of the outside of a lemon. There is also banana yellow.

• Olive is the color of an olive in a jar (not ripe olives). Another good olive is the color of ripe avocado flesh, which is much like the color of the bottom of the abdomen of most blue-winged olives, although that can depend on the time of year they are hatching. (Early- and late-season BWOs tend to be a darker green than mid-summer ones.) Dark olive is the color of an army blanket. Well-cooked green beans are yet another shade of olive, as are cooked lima beans.

• Tan is the color of a paper grocery bag.

• Ginger is the color of the ground spice.

• Gray is the color of the bark of a mountain ash tree.

• Rust is the color of a rusty nail.

• Cream is the color of pure dairy cream.

• Red is stop-sign red.

• Black is the color of chimney soot.

• Orange is the color of ripe orange peel.

• Brown is the most difficult of all, since there are so many shades. As it's best to relate the shade of brown to some common natural object we all have access to, mahogany is a good place to start.

It's my belief that if we can relate the colors we see in the insects we are trying to imitate to some of those listed above, there will be a lot less confusion as to what colors to use when tying or describing the flies we see. By mixing dyes and pinches of different colors of dubbing, we can arrive at a near perfect color match for any insect we are trying to imitate.

Each of these colors contains varying amounts of pigments that result in the final color we perceive. The primary colors of yellow, blue, and red are found in some combination in everything we look at except in pure white. What we see are those pigments that are reflected from an object. For example, a red object is reflecting red rays of the color spectrum more than others.

When it comes to aquatic insects, it's easy to misidentify the colors of the natural. Just as the dyes we use to change the color of a material contain many different pigments, so do the insects. To prove this to yourself, pick up a live adult mayfly next time you're on your favorite stream. A blue-winged olive is a good one to start with. Examine the bottom of its abdomen with your eyes almost closed, looking through your eyelashes, and you will see other shades of color besides the pale green of the belly. Faint shades of cream, yellow, and light gray suddenly appear as if out of nowhere. When you mix your dubbing to imitate the natural, experiment with pinches of all four colors until you arrive at the proper shade, remembering that when the dubbing gets wet, it will be a little darker. Also keep in mind that the adult's body never gets wet. Your dubbing when wet—or after it has been treated with a fly waterproofing agent—must be the same color as the natural's dry body. This is where a camera and a 50-millimeter macro lens become very important.

Close-up of blue-winged olive body

Speaking of photography, have you ever noticed that many photos of mayflies in nearly all the books and articles about fly tying and hatches never show us the color of the bottom of the fly? It's the most important color, since it's what the trout sees. We all have a tendency to catch a bug and look at it from the top down. The trout, however, always looks up.

Photo of bottom of blue-winged olive

Water quality can affect the color of the body of an insect. Another variable is the time of year when you capture a bug. Early-season insects are often darker than those in midsummer. And colors can differ depending on the part of the country or even the stream. Fly tiers and writers should always indicate the time of year and the stream when describing how to tie a fly or mix the dubbing for it, and they should include sharp close-up photos to clearly demonstrate everything about the insect.

Photo of top of blue-winged olive

CHAPTER 8

Hackle Names and Colors

When it comes to hackles and body feathers, color names are a different ball game from body color names. Some of the terms still used today to describe hackle color go back more than two hundred years. Today's genetically engineered bird skins have colors that were unheard of just forty years ago, so there are a lot of new color names to describe both natural and dyed necks and saddles. The names given to the hues of body feathers on some newer crossbred birds are much the same as for game bird necks and saddles. At least there is some consistency in this.

Most of today's hackle farms are turning out dry-fly capes and saddles with about twenty-one different natural colors, several of them due to crossbreeding. And crossbreeding is a tricky game to play, because recessive genes often rear their heads in later generations, which can produce some fantastic new colors that can be very difficult or impossible to re-create.

Jacqueline Wakeford wrote a book titled *Flytying Tools and Materials* (Lyons and Burford, 1991), which gives one of the best historical descriptions (with photos) of hackle and feather colors that I know of. If you wish to learn a little of the history of some of the hackle names and their colors, it's a valuable resource.

Historically, the basic hackle colors are as follows:

• White is often more of an ivory or off-white. Pure white is not rare, but it's not what I'd call common.

• Light cream is a little darker than ivory.

• Light ginger is often called honey ginger, but lighter in color than real honey. But then, that depends on the honey farm, as some honey is much darker than others.

• Medium ginger is closer to the color of honey.

• Dark ginger is more of a light tan, somewhat like dark honey.

• Light red is really light brown by today's standards.

• Medium red is medium brown by today's standards.

• Dark red formerly was often called red game, but today it is simply called brown and is slightly darker than medium brown. It's a suitable substitute for Coachman brown.

• Very dark red formerly was called chocolate but today is called Coachman brown.

• Black—what can I say? Black is black.

• Light badger has a black strip along a black center quill, with the hackle fibers being of a lighter color, often a light ginger. A very light-colored feather, almost white, is often called silver badger.

• Medium badger can have a little wider black center strip, the lighter hackle fibers often have black tips, and the surrounding hackle fibers are about a shade darker than the light badger.

• Dark badger has a little wider black strip, and the ends of the hackle fibers are prominently black tipped with an almost medium ginger midsection.

• Furnace has a black center that is almost half the length of each hackle fiber and looks more like a streamer feather than dry-fly hackle.

There are three shades of furnace—dark, medium, and light—and all have a black strip along the black quill.

• Coch-y-bondhu is a very dark furnace.

• Grizzly was originally called cuckoo, according to Wakeford. When I lived on a farm in Iowa, we called these birds barred Plymouth Rocks. The common color name today of grizzly has nothing to do with the bear of the same name. A grizzly feather is best described as creamy white with black chevron stripes across the center quill and hackle fibers. The most common grizzly feathers have a black chevron shape. The best ones have horizontal barring across the quill. The colors range from very light with sparse medium gray barring to a light gray with denser black barring. If you can find a neck or saddle with feathers that are nearly white with black horizontal barring, buy it! As a result of some selective crossbreeding, it's not rare to find barred necks and saddles ranging in color from creamy white to dark ginger.

• Cree is one of the most difficult to find of all feather colors and is the most discussed and cussed. Most people ignore the fact that there are several color shades of cree, just as with gingers, duns, and browns. A cree feather looks much like a grizzly at first glance, but closer examination will show that instead of just a white feather with black barring, a cree is some shade of light cream to dark ginger with white, black, and brown barring. Light necks sometimes have no black barring at all yet still are called cree. Some say that a true cree's bars progress up from the butt as black on the bottom, then white or cream, and then brown. Others say it's brown first, and still others say it's white first. I say it doesn't matter to the trout or the fly, since once the hackle is wound around the hook, no one can tell.

• Dun is the word given to a feather that is some shade of gray. Most of these birds are descendants of an old breed called Andalusian blue, and I suspect this is where the term blue dun originated. Over time, modern crossbreeding techniques have led to a wide range of hues:

—Smoky dun is a very light gray.

—Medium dun is a plain gray, about the same color as muskrat underfur.

—Dark dun is a charcoal gray.

—Honey dun is a gray with hints of the color of honey. It can be light, medium, or dark.

—Chocolate dun is a gray with noticeable hints of brown. It's darker than honey dun.

—Sandy dun is a light ginger with a light gray cast.

—Bronze dun is basically a medium ginger with a medium gray cast.

—Rusty dun is a medium brown feather with hints of medium gray.

Finding a neck or saddle to exactly match one that you have used up can be very difficult, especially for a color with many varieties of shades, such as ginger or brown. When they find a rare natural-color neck, many tiers will simply buy it and save it as a color match for a dyeing job or preserve it in a plastic sleeve to impress their friends.

If you want to learn more than you need to know about the many breeds of chickens, do a Google or Ask Jeeves search on chicken breeds on your computer. You'll find ten pages or more of listings on just about every living chicken in the world. One of my favorite websites is www.ansi.okstate.edu/poultry/chickens, which describes the birds and their colors, talks about their origin, and includes color pictures of most of them.

Not much of the above has a great deal to do with necks or backs from different game hens or game birds, however, all of which have even more variance in their colors. Where the game birds live, which sex they are, and their diet all greatly affect the color of their body feathers. Many of these birds have distinctive mottling on their neck and body feathers, which is very useful in tying soft-hackle flies, as beards and pulled-back legs on nymphs, and for some streamer patterns. The most common mottled colors are brown, tan, and gray. The darker part of the mottling is often black or dark brown, and it can be a combination of both black and brown on a lighter-colored feather.

Of course, most of the above colors can be dyed to a darker shade, which can produce some outstanding feathers for specific patterns. But be careful that you always test-dye a single feather before you drop the entire skin into the dye bath. Most importantly, keep a natural feather along with the dyed feather so that a few years down the road, if you want to re-create the same color shade, you will know what you started with.

There is a tremendous amount of history connected to fly tying, and in particular, the feathers used. Some exotic feathers are no longer legally available, some are very expensive, and some are extremely rare even though the price may not indicate this. It's much easier today than it was fifty years ago to find the exact color and quality of feather you may need for a specific pattern, thanks to the hackle farms that are producing quality feathers in colors we couldn't even dream about just thirty years ago. Many of these farms have mastered the art of dyeing feathers for color consistency, and some dye manufacturers are producing dyes just for us. Sort of gives you a warm, fuzzy feeling, doesn't it?

New Materials
and Patterns

CHAPTER 9

New Quill Material

I think I may have solved a problem for a lot of tiers who would like to tie quill-bodied flies but haven't been able to find the right feathers (strung Chinese rooster neck hackle) or get the quill body and black lace capes from Whiting Farms. Not all fly shops carry these Whiting products. There are also the problems of cracking and splitting and what some folks feel is the fragile nature of the material. Coupled with all this is the fact that avian influenza, or bird flu, is ravaging chickens in much of Asia and has now spread to the Middle East. At the time of this writing more than two hundred people have died of it in some Asian countries. Our government is becoming alarmed about the possibility of a pandemic occurrence in the United States and other nations outside of Asia. It could become a very serious problem. And it will probably mean an embargo will be placed on poultry and any kind of poultry parts, maybe even including feathers, coming from any Asiatic country. So if you have a supply of strung Chinese neck hackle for tying quill-bodied flies, be careful with your backcast!

A major portion of my income is generated by tying flies for Mike Clark's South Creek Ltd. in Lyons, Colorado. Most of the flies I sell to Mike are quill-bodied patterns that I have developed over the past fifteen or twenty years. And my supply of strung Chinese rooster neck hackle is beginning to run a little low, so I've been agonizing over what to use if I run out and can't get any more. Whiting's quill body capes and black lace necks are very good, but they're a little pricey when compared with the cost of a couple pounds of strung Chinese rooster neck hackle. I did a lot of looking and experimenting and hadn't been able to find anything remotely close to the above products. That is, until one day when I walked into a popular local fly shop, the Front Range Angler, in Boulder, Colorado, to buy a small package of white turkey flats. I was working on an article about wing-post material and wanted to photograph the difference between a turkey T-base feather and a turkey flat, which are two distinct types of feathers that come from different parts of the bird, though most fly shops label the T-base feathers as turkey flats. T-base feathers come from the neck and breast of the turkey, whereas flats come from the back or saddle portion of the body. T-base feathers are only about two inches long and have very dense fibers all the way to the tips, which are pretty much straight across. A segment of a T-base feather makes a perfect wing post on any parachute pattern of any size. It's lighter in weight than a corresponding bundle of calf hair and much easier to manage. Flats are seven or more inches long, with a lot of maraboulike fibers along the main stem and only a few straight fibers near the tip.

These straight fibers gradually become very wispy about one fourth of an inch or more from their ends, making them useless for wing posts on parachutes.

T-base and flat feathers

While handling these two feather types, I noticed that the center quill of a turkey flat extends all the way to the very tip of the feather. Just the right sized quill for a size 22 or even 24 mayfly body. I also noticed that the taper of the quill was progressively larger toward the butt of the feather, much more so than on a Chinese rooster neck hackle. I should be able to create a body on any size hook with only one quill. This would mean much more flotation from a greater amount of pith in the center of the quill on larger fly sizes such as the Green and Brown Drakes. Because of the greater diameter, I would not have

Size 18, 16, 14, and 12 dry flies (all Baetis *green): four flies from the same quill*

to dub an underbody before winding a wild turkey biot for the body of the fly. Biot-bodied flies look real nice, but to get the right body silhouette, you need to dub an underbody before wrapping the biot on any fly of size 14 or larger. It appeared as if I would be able to tie at least four different-size flies from the same feather, provided I could strip all the fluff and fibers from the quill with little effort and end up with a quill that wouldn't crack or split when I tried to wind it around a hook shank. And more importantly, how well would the stripped quills accept water-based dyes such as Rit and Veniard? Another question I wanted to answer was, how much pressure would the quill take before it began to flatten as I wound it around the hook?

Turkey Flat Preparation

I occasionally have a moment of epiphany, and this was one in capital letters. After experimenting with the turkey flats, I found that they are easily burned in a fifty-fifty mixture of hot tap water and Clorox and readily accept a dye. The best part is that turkey flats are very inexpensive, and they don't flatten or crack as they are wound around the hook. You can still achieve the waxy light-reflective quality needed to match the natural's appearance, and the segmentation effect from the wound quill is quite obvious. They do everything for your fly that a stripped and dyed rooster hackle quill will do, maybe even better.

Here's how to burn turkey flats before dyeing them:

1. Bundle about twenty flat feathers at their tips with a small rubber band.

2. Spray with Formula 409 liquid cleaner and let soak for about ten minutes to degrease, then rinse in warm water. This will also prevent the marabou fibers from matting together, which would keep the Clorox solution from working down to the quill.

3. Make a fifty-fifty mixture of hot tap water and Clorox.

4. Fill a clear glass with plain water to use for inspection.

5. In another glass, mix two tablespoons of baking soda in warm water for neutralizing the Clorox when you're done burning.

6. Immerse the butts of the flats as far as they will go into the Clorox solution, and constantly agitate in an up-and-down motion.

7. When they begin to look clean, rinse under the faucet and place them in the inspection glass to see if anything is left on the quills. If a few stubs remain, put the clump back into the Clorox solution for a few seconds more, and then repeat the inspection.

8. Once the bases of the quills are clean, remove the rubber band from the tips and wind it around the butts.

9. Immerse the tips in the same solution and agitate until they have been cleaned of all fibers. Be careful here—the quills near the tips are very thin, and too much time in the Clorox solution will begin to destroy the enamel coating. This will cause the quill to split as you wind it around the hook shank.

10. When you are satisfied that the burning process is complete, rinse the quills thoroughly, and then put them in the glass of baking soda and water for about ten minutes.

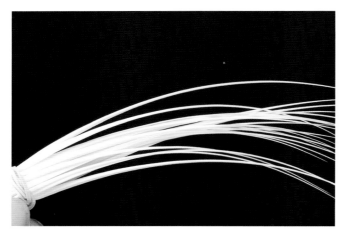

11. Rinse until the quills no longer feel slick. Dye the quills any color you choose.

12. You can use the dye recipes given in my book *Dying and Bleaching Natural Fly-Tying Materials* (Lyons Press, 2004) to create the colors you need for body material on all of your flies.

So, do you need to tie half a dozen quill-bodied Blue-Winged Olives? Starting with the smallest size you will need, count out six sets of hooks, hackles, wings, and only six quills! If you need to tie them from sizes 22 through 14 (five hook sizes), that makes thirty flies from six quills. How's that for economy? Now you no longer need to use two quills on hooks of size 16 and larger to simulate the correct body silhouette and taper because of the increasing diameter of the turkey flat quill. The tip of the quill you will use should be about the same diameter as the eye of the hook you are using.

If you need only size 22s, bundle the remaining portion of the cut quills and label them with a piece of masking tape indicating what portion you have used, such as –22.

Selection of dry flies (duns, parachutes, spinners, and drakes) tied with turkey flat quills

Here are the tying instructions for any quill-bodied dry fly using stripped and dyed white turkey flats:

1. Attach the tying thread to the hook about one hook-gap space behind the eye, wind to the beginning of the bend, clip off the tag, and take two more turns of thread over the last turn to create a tiny thread bump.

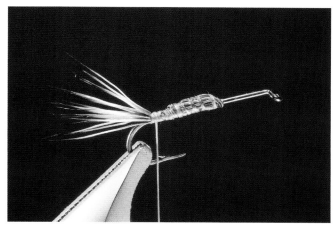

2. Tie the tailing fibers onto the hook immediately in front of the thread bump. This will cock them up slightly, much like the natural's tails. The cocked-up tails will also function as a bit of an airfoil, helping ensure that your fly will land upright.

3. Lash the butts down toward the thread starting point, then lift the butts and clip them off even with the thread starting point. Save one hook-gap space for wings, hackle collar, and head.

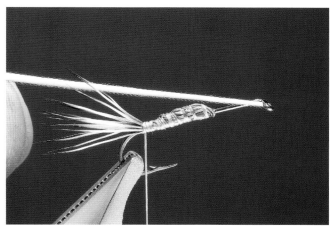

4. Clip the tip of a stripped and dyed turkey flat at a point where the remaining end is slightly smaller in diameter than the hook eye. Discard the fine tip.

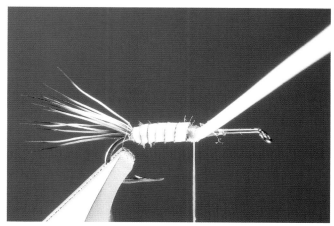

5. Tie the remainder of the quill to the hook, with the clipped end even with the clipped tailing butts. This will become the shoulder of the body.

6. Lash the quill down toward the bend of the hook with very firm turns of thread, stopping the thread wraps just short of the last turn of thread holding the tailing.

7. Bring the thread forward to the shoulder and leave it hang.

8. Wind the quill forward in tightly nesting turns, and tie off on top of the hook with six or seven very firm turns of thread.

9. Lift the butt and clip it off at an angle.

10. Cover the clipped butt with several turns of thread to create a smooth area for the wings and hackle collar.

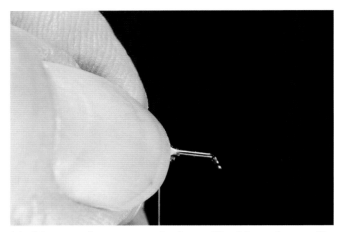

11. You may have to smash the quill a bit on larger flies such as drake patterns by pressing down on the clipped butt with your thumbnail or the back of your scissors. I don't recommend using 8/0 threads on large drake patterns; 4/0 works the best, because it has more of a flat surface than finer threads.

12. Select a pair of dyed hen hackle tips (color to match the natural), measure for length, and tie them onto the hook with their tips to the rear, just in front of the shoul-

der. Save enough room behind the wings for two or three turns of hackle on fly sizes 16 and 14. Save enough room for four or five turns behind the wings on fly sizes 12 and larger. Stand the wings up and divide with one figure-eight wrap of thread.

13. Select a dry-fly hackle, clip the butt fibers, tie onto the hook in your favorite manner, and wind. Then tie off the hackle, clip off the tip, whip-finish, and apply a tiny drop of head lacquer.

The stripped and dyed turkey flat quills are much more durable than rooster neck butt hackle, because the enamel-like coating on the quill is much thicker and seems to be a little more pliable. With all the turkey farms in the United States, we should have an unending supply of white turkey flats—unless the bird flu hits this country and infects our turkey farms too. Then we'll all have to tie dubbed-body flies. Stock up on white turkey flats!

CHAPTER 10

Working with Bugskin

This may read like a blatant advertisement for a commercial product, but I've been tying with this stuff for a few years now, and surprisingly, it is not readily available in some parts of the country. Bugskin is a by-product of the fancy leather goods industry. You know, those $400 purses that your wife covets? Or that beautiful leather jacket you saw in a high-end men's store, but then you figured you could get another fly rod and reel for what the jacket cost?

Chuck Furimsky has a fancy leather goods shop at a ski lodge in Seven Springs, Pennsylvania. He's also an avid fly fisher and tier, and like most of us, he is always on the lookout for something new to use for tying. As in the manufacture of most things, there is always some excess leather material that is usually tossed out. A few years ago, Chuck grabbed a handful of this material and began playing around with it. His first attempts were at tying up some crayfish and stonefly nymph patterns that were not only very effective, but extremely durable as well. I came across the material at a fly-fishing show in New Jersey a few years ago, where Chuck was marketing it as Bugskin (not to be confused with buckskin). It comes in a wide variety of colors, from jet black to just about any pop-star vibrance you could imagine. The ones that interested me were the bronze, light tan, and black. Beetles and Buckskin Nymphs!

Finally, here is a shellback material for beetles that does not self-destruct after three or four fish. Plus it's a natural material, and I do have a penchant for using only natural materials on my flies. There's already enough synthetic stuff in the environment that will still be there thousands of years from now, and I don't want to add to it by using synthetics on the flies I leave hanging in trees and bushes.

Bugskin is packaged in patches that are about 3 by 5 inches, with one or two patches in a zipped plastic hang bag. One side of the leather patch is split or rough, and the other side is slick or shiny. And you need to understand that as with many things natural, there is a grain or stretch factor that goes in only one direction. When you cut the patch into strips for use on flies, if you cut with the grain, the leather strip will shrink after fishing and get narrower. You can avoid this by always cutting the strips to be used across the grain. The best way to determine which way the grain goes is to hold a corner between the thumb and forefinger of each hand and gently pull. Notice how much stretch there is when you do this. Then try the same on two different corners.

Lots of stretch (with the grain)

Not much stretch (across the grain)

Some common colors of Bugskin

Black and Bronze Bugskin Winged Beetles

I've written about the Bugskin Winged Beetle a couple of times, most notably in my book *Advanced Fly Tying* (Lyons Press, 2001). Refer to it for more details, but following is the recipe:

Bugskin Winged Beetle

Hook:	Your favorite dry-fly hook, sizes 18–12
Thread:	Danville's black 6/0
Wing tips:	Pair of medium dun hen hackle tips
Shellback:	Strip of Bugskin, width equal to hook-gap space
Dubbing:	Brown for Bronze Beetle or black for Black Beetle
Hackle:	Palmered brown for Bronze Beetle or black for Black Beetle

The Buckskin Nymph is a pattern that has been around for a very long time and is particularly effective in tailwaters. The original pattern called for a narrow strip of buckskin wrapped around the hook shank to simulate a nymph larva. Terry Hellekson describes the original pattern in his wonderful reference book *Popular Fly Patterns* (Peregrine Smith, 1976) as follows:

Buckskin Nymph

Hook:	Mustad 3906B, sizes 6–12
Thread:	Black
Tip:	Flat gold tinsel
Tail:	Soft brown hackle fibers
Underbody:	Lead wire and thread
Outer body:	Narrow ribbon of buckskin wrapped on edge

Most of the flies of this pattern I see in shops today have omitted both the gold tag and the soft brown hackle tail and substituted chamois for the body. The problem with using this material for the body is that when cut into narrow strips, chamois becomes very fragile and often pulls apart when you try to wrap it around the hook—especially when tying smaller versions (18s and 20s), which have become extremely effective.

Bugskin to the rescue! It's available in a color that perfectly matches buckskin, and it is much stronger than chamois even when cut into strips thin enough to tie a size 22! You will need a thin steel straightedge and a very sharp X-acto blade to cut such narrow strips, however. Place the Bugskin shiny side up on the back of a writing tablet, put the steel ruler on top of the Bugskin, and very firmly hold it down as you slice off a narrow strip. *Note:* Be very careful not to cut off a fingertip as you do this!

Cutting Bugskin strip

Simple Bugskin (Buckskin) Nymph

Hook:	Your favorite nymph hook (I use dry-fly hooks, preferring to put weight on my leader, which keeps the fly just above the rocks, not among them)
Thread:	Danville's black 6/0
Tag:	None
Tail:	None
Body:	Thin strip of light tan Bugskin

1. Place the hook in the vise, and attach the tying thread one hook-eye space behind the eye. Wind almost to the end of the shank. If you go all the way to the end, you risk having a wrap or two of black thread showing behind the Bugskin strip.

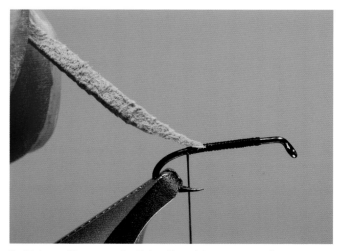

2. Trim off one end of the Bugskin at an angle

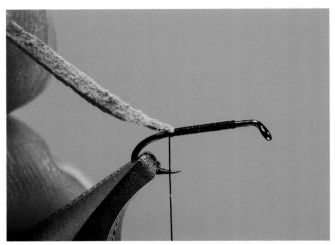

3. Tie the trimmed point on top of the hook, with the angled cut to the rear, with three or four turns of thread.

4. Bring the thread forward to hang one hook-eye space behind the eye.

5. Carefully wrap the Bugskin strip forward in tightly nesting turns, stopping one hook-eye space behind the eye. Tie off on top of the hook and clip off the excess. Whip-finish and apply a tiny drop of head lacquer to the head only.

I love it when I get an order for several dozen of this pattern. It's essentially a two-piece fly: thread and Bugskin.

If you are always looking for some new stuff to tie with, try a standard mayfly nymph using Bugskin as the body material and a darker strip for the wing pad. A few tail fibers, a fuzzy dubbed thorax, and perhaps a soft-hackle beard, and you can tie indestructible nymphs that will feel more natural in the trout's mouth.

Now from the inventor of Bugskin come tying steps for some patterns that have proven very effective if tied to Chuck's instructions. Not only do these flies look good to both the fisher and the fish, but they also have a more realistic feel, so the fish don't spit them out, and they are nearly indestructible.

Bugskin "Walk and Roll" Nymph

Hook:	Your favorite curved-shank down-eye nymph hook
Thread:	Tan 6/0 or 8/0
Tail:	Small clump of hen back fibers, length to equal hook gap
Underbody:	Fibers from bathroom cotton ball
Shellback:	Bugskin strip
Rib:	Copper wire
Abdomen:	Any kind of sparkle dubbing
Wing pad:	Darker Bugskin strip
Thorax:	Darker than abdomen sparkle dubbing
Legs:	Hen hackle fibers on each side, length to hook point

1. This first step came from an idea of George Harvey's to create a more realistically shaped nymph body. Attach tying thread to the hook about a hook-eye space behind the eye, and wind to just over the hook point.

2. Loosely dub cotton fibers and wind onto the hook to create a fat cigar shape.

3. Soak dubbed underbody with head lacquer or fingernail polish, allow to dry a little, and flatten with flat needlenose pliers (not grooved). Use your forefinger to stroke stray fibers into shape.

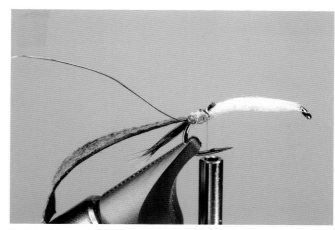

4. Tie in a small clump of hen hackle fibers for the tail.

5. Select a Bugskin color and cut a strip about as wide as the hook gap. Cut one end to an arrow shape, and tie it in by its tip with the dull side up.

6. Tie in an 8-inch length of copper wire on your side of the hook.

7. Begin the abdomen dubbing just behind the wire rib tie-in so that the first turn of wire over the shellback and abdomen does not go over the tailing.

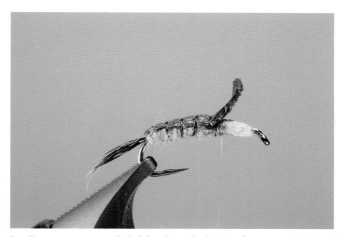

8. Create a tapered dubbed underbody for two-thirds of the rear of the hook, pull the shellback forward, and tie down. Spiral-wrap the wire forward to create evenly spaced body segments, tie off, and trim off excess wire. Tug on the shellback and clip off excess.

9. Next you will make a wing-pad Bugskin strip with a broad arrow shape. Select a darker-colored Bugskin for the wing pad, and cut a strip slightly wider than the abdomen shellback. Cut a slightly broader arrow shape, and tie on with the dull side up immediately on top of the shellback cutoff.

10. Apply darker dubbing for the thorax, no larger in diameter than the shoulder of the body. Pull the wing-pad thorax forward, and tie down slightly behind the eye. Add hen fibers on each side of the hook. Trim off the hen hackle butts and Bugskin strip to form a head, whip-finish, and apply a drop of head lacquer to the head. Carefully brush head lacquer over the Bugskin shellback and wing pad and set aside to dry. This completes your Bugskin "Walk and Roll" Nymph.

One of the most realistic crayfish patterns I have ever seen is one that Chuck has created using his Bugskin. I can't think of a trout stream that doesn't have a healthy population of crayfish, yet it seems to be a pattern that is seldom fished and is not stocked in all fly shops. I'm thinking maybe it looks too much like a bass lure. But that's OK—use it for bass as well! We do it with streamers.

Bugskin Crayfish	
Hook:	Any 2X strong straight-eye streamer hook, sizes 4–10
Thread:	Tan or olive 6/0
Antennae:	Small clump of fox squirrel, length to equal two to three hook-gap spaces
Carapace:	Mottled brown Bugskin cut to shape (see parts photo below, but cut it a little longer than you need; measure to be a little longer than the entire hook and trim tail to length after completing step 11)
Eyes:	Two 20-pound-test lengths of mono-filament, burned and painted with black enamel
Dubbing:	Tan or olive
Pincers:	Glue rough sides together to make two pairs with shiny sides both top and bottom (see parts photo below)
Rib:	Copper wire
Hackle:	Brown dyed grizzly

Left to right: carapace (note hole near tail), mono eyes, pincers, grizzly, wire

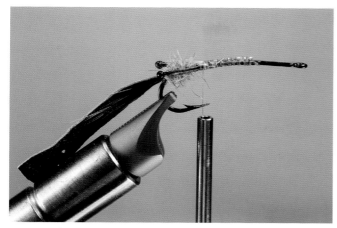

1. Attach tying thread at midshank, and firmly wind slightly into the bend to angle antennae down.

2. Tie in a small clump of fox squirrel for antennae, and allow to curve into hook bend slightly.

3. Tie in carapace by its tip, with the shiny side down.

4. Apply a small ball of dubbing to separate eyes, which are tied in next.

5. Flatten eye-post rods with flat needlenose pliers, and tie in so that the eyes extend almost beyond the end of the bend.

6. Tie pincers on each side to remain horizontal and extend beyond the hook bend by about one hook-gap space.

7. Dub to cover pincer tie-down and to create some bulk to the thorax area. Tie on wire rib, and hackle feather by its butt, concave side forward, and continue to dub for a distance slightly farther than the hook-gap space.

8. Palmer-wrap the hackle, then tie off and trim the tip. Spiral-wrap wire through the hackle (keep the remainder!), and continue to dub to the hook eye.

9. Stretch the carapace toward the hook eye to determine hole placement, and make a hole to accept the hook eye.

10. Carefully apply contact cement or equivalent to underside of carapace and top of body. Allow to dry slightly, pull the carapace over the body toward the eye, and press into shape with your fingers.

11. Firmly wind copper wire over the body to create prominent segments, tie off, and trim away wire and thread. Apply a small drop of head lacquer to thread finish, and pull the Bugskin tail over the hook eye. This completes your Bugskin Crayfish.

CHAPTER 11

Tying with Coq de Leon

The first time I saw coq de Leon feathers was while visiting Tom Whiting's farm near Delta, Colorado, a few years ago. We were discussing the lack of tailing side feathers on today's genetically engineered necks when he pulled a few coq de Leon saddles from a pile of exotic pelts on his desk. "What do you think of these?" he asked. I was ecstatic about the quality of the feather fibers and the magnificent coloration and speckling in each saddle. I immediately bought half a dozen light-colored saddles so I could dye them to the tailing colors I needed on dry flies.

It wasn't until I had dyed one saddle to ginger and another to light dun that I noticed the butt feathers on each of the coq de Leon saddles are of a different appearance. Some are totally black with beautiful greenish purple highlights, and some are mottled much like an enormous partridge breast feather. My mind flashed forward to bass bug wings, tarpon wings, and Matuka flies tied with these beautiful feathers. I've been playing around with dyeing some of them in different colors to see what I could come up with in the way of usable feathers for extralarge streamer patterns.

By large, I mean streamers on a Mustad 79580 size 2 hook or larger. The butt feathers from a coq de Leon saddle are both long and wide enough to tie streamers on saltwater hooks up to 5/0. There are many smaller feathers for tying smaller flies.

Coq de Leon translates to mean "rooster from Leon." Leon is a region in Spain where this bird is the earliest-known chicken to be raised for fly-tying use. It has wonderfully shiny feathers with very long, stiff hackle fibers. The saddles are perfect for tailing on most normal-size mayflies, containing feathers with hackle fibers long enough to tie tailing on a size 10 dry fly. But the humoral tract feathers, commonly known as pardo, contain the longest, stiffest hackle fibers you can find anywhere. They're so stiff you can almost hurt yourself with them. The humoral tract is a narrow patch of feathers from the shoulder of the rooster. The natural colors of this bird range from near white to light brown, with fine speckling or dots on each hackle fiber. The hackle fibers are almost a perfect match to the segmentation markings on a mayfly's tail fibers, to simulate the joints in a crane fly's legs, or to give the impression of a fluttering insect. Tom Whiting of Whiting Farms in Delta, Colorado, has been working on developing these birds for several years. Both the saddles and tailing packs (humoral tracts) are available in most fly shops that have good supplies of fly-tying materials. The feathers from both can be dyed, but it takes a little longer to achieve the desired color simply because the hackle fibers are much harder than those found on the standard dry-fly neck or saddle.

Disclaimer: I am not employed by Whiting Farms. It's just damn good material, and I think you all ought to know about it!

Coq de Leon saddle feather

Coq de Leon humoral tract

Coq de Leon saddle

Coq de Leon pardo feather

Streamers

I'll give two examples of streamers tied from coq de Leon feathers: a brown-dyed Dark Spruce Streamer and a ginger-dyed Matuka-style streamer. Once you lay eyes on these beautiful capes, I'm sure you can come up with a few more patterns for saltwater fishing as well, such as Deceivers and other tarpon and striper patterns. There are two problems with using coq de Leon saddle butts for streamer tying: First, there aren't more than half a dozen flies that can be tied in this large size from each saddle, and second, no two saddles are exactly alike. The latter isn't a crucial problem, since we are always looking for variations in feather quality and markings when tying streamers. Basically, the butt feathers are either mottled or they're not. If they're not, they are iridescent black. Use a 0X tippet to fish these streamers where you know there is a big trout!

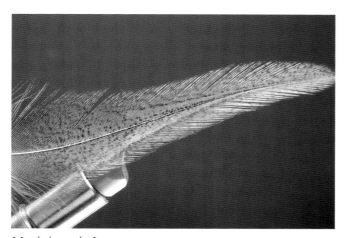

Mottled coq de Leon

Iridescent coq de Leon

Coq de Leon Dark Spruce Streamer	
Hook:	Mustad 79580 size 2 or larger
Thread:	Black monocord
Tail:	Dozen or more peacock eye tips
Body:	Rear two-thirds: four-strand red floss; front third: six to eight strands of peacock herl
Wing:	Two pairs of well-marked dark badger feathers
Collar:	One well-marked dark badger feather

Note: This streamer is often more effective if it is weighted by wrapping lead substitute wire of the same diameter as the hook shank in the area that the peacock thorax will cover. Save at least one hook-gap space behind the eye for wing tie-down and hackle collar.

1. Start the thread on the hook about a hook-gap space behind the eye, wrap to the end of the hook shank, and bring the thread forward to the starting point.

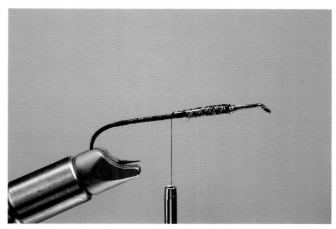

2. Add lead substitute wire if desired, beginning one hook-gap space behind the eye and wrapping to the rear for a distance of one-third the hook-shank length.

3. Cover the lead wraps with tying thread in open spirals back and forward at least twice. Liberally coat with head lacquer.

4. Tie in about a dozen peacock eye herl tips at the hook bend, bind to the shank up to the rear of the lead wraps, and snip off the butts. Tail length should extend beyond the end of the shank by two hook-gap spaces.

5. Tie in four-strand floss immediately behind the lead wraps, and wind the floss to the rear and then forward as many times as it takes to create a smoothly tapered body up to the lead wraps.

6. Select six to eight strands of peacock herl, and tie them in by their tips immediately on top of the front of the lead wraps.

7. Lash the peacock to the rear of the lead wraps, wind the peacock around the thread, wind the rope forward, and tie it off on top of the hook just behind the hook

eye. This last is done to raise the level on which the wings will be tied.

8. Select two pairs of well-marked dark badger feathers, two from each side of the butt. Match the tips and cut the butts off at a point where the remaining feather is twice the length of the hook.

9. Tie the butts on top of the hook, and make them lie as flat to the hook as possible. Feather tips should flare outward.

10. Select one well-marked dark badger feather, and cut the butt at a point where the black center will match the wing feathers. Lash it to the top of the hook with the shiny side forward, and wind forward. Stroke each wrap to the rear.

11. Wrap the thread to lean the collar slightly backward, whip-finish, and apply two or three coats of thick head lacquer. This completes your Coq de Leon Dark Spruce Streamer.

Tan Coq de Leon Matuka

Hook:	Mustad 79580, size 2 or larger
Thread:	Tan monocord
Weight:	Lead substitute wire
Rib:	Gold double-strand braided tinsel
Body:	Tan yarn
Wing:	Two mottled coq de Leon saddle butt feathers
Collar:	Two mottled coq de Leon saddle butt feathers

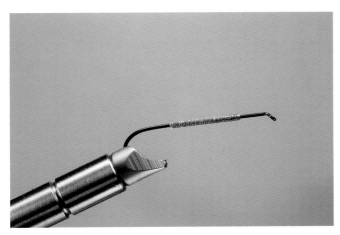

1. Wrap the hook with lead substitute wire from one hook-gap space behind the eye to just above the hook point.

2. Attach tying thread, spiral-wrap twice up and down over the wire, and bring the thread to hang just behind the wire wraps. Liberally coat this assembly with head lacquer.

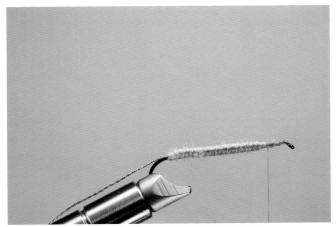

3. Attach the gold ribbing just behind the wire wraps.

4. Attach the yarn just behind the wire wraps, wind forward, and tie down on top of the hook just in front of the wire wraps. Clip off excess yarn.

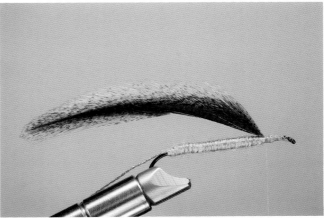

5. Trim the butts of the wing feathers to allow bare quill for tie-down, and clean the bottom of the feathers to just in front of the hook point. The shiny side of each feather should face out.

6. Tie the matched wings on top of the hook in front of the wire wraps.

7. Moisten the wings and separate the fibers into a series of small Vs.

8. Hold the wings up and take one full turn of ribbing over the yarn body.

9. Pull the tail of the wings tight to the rear, and begin ribbing the feathers in open spiral wraps to the top of the hook.

10. Tie off the ribbing on top of the hook in front of the shoulder.

11. Trim the hackle collar butts, tie them to the top of the hook in front of the wing with the shiny side forward, and wind both forward at the same time. Stroke each wrap to the rear.

12. Tie off the tips on top of the hook, trim off the tips, and whip-finish.

13. Apply two or three coats of thick head lacquer to complete your Tan Coq de Leon Matuka.

Hovering Crane Flies!

One of my mottos is "Assumptions are always danger-ous." I try very hard never to assume anything about anything. But I got caught up in violating that credo when I thought I was observing a size 10 or 12 Western Red Quill hatch. It kept me from catching trout during a few weeks each summer for nearly five years. I could see those big brown mayflies flying overhead in their mating flights and then watch clouds of them hovering low over some broken water in what I assumed was an egg-laying drop. Twelve- to fourteen-inch brown trout would actually launch themselves out of the water to grab these big morsels in midair! I tried everything from large March Browns to Brown Drakes in an attempt to match this hatch, but I couldn't get a strike. I was never able to find a natural on the water to net, and that puzzled and frustrated me.

I sat down on a large rock late one afternoon in a state of total frustration and just watched the bugs and the fish as I tried to figure out what to do to solve the problem. As I was lighting a cigar, one of the insects landed on the boulder next to me. It was a brown crane fly! Suddenly everything made perfect sense. A crane fly trails its rear pair of legs behind it when in flight, giving the visual impression of the tail fibers of a mayfly. Long brown legs and a skinny brown body with light medium dun wings made these flying insects appear as if they were large mayflies in flight.

But how does one tie a fly that actually hovers? There's a trick the late Charlie Brooks showed me years ago to fool big brown trout that come out of the water to eat large dragonflies on the Madison River in Yellow-stone Park. He tied a 2-foot length of monofilament sewing thread to the bend of the hook of a large dragon-fly pattern and attached a small treble hook to the end of the mono. He then abruptly choked his cast in such a way that the fly would stop short of the grass on the far streamside bank and the treble hook would sail over it and snag in the grass. The dancing fly would fool even the biggest and wariest brown trout. The sewing thread broke on the strike, and Charlie had his fish minus one tiny treble hook dangling in the grass. A small price to pay for a large brown trout. My problem was, no grass!

It took me two years to figure this one out. The mate-rials to tie the Hovering Crane Fly are readily available except for the hackle. I wanted some very stiff brown hackle with no web whose fibers were more than an inch long. Coq de Leon to the rescue!

My version of this fly doesn't really hover, but it does sit well up above the water and can be twitched or skit-tered quite easily. The following pattern is the result of dozens of tries to achieve the desired effect.

Hovering Crane Fly

Hook:	Mustad 94831, sizes 14–12
Thread:	Danville's brown 6/0, number 47
Tail:	One pardo feather with center tip clipped out
Body:	No body material is needed
Wings:	Pair of slender light dun hen hackle tips
Rear body:	Two pardo feathers tied shiny side up
Front body and hackle collar:	
	Two pardo feathers tied shiny side down

1. Select five pardo feathers whose hackle fibers are equal in length.

2. Place the hook in the vise, attach the tying thread immediately behind the eye, and wrap to the beginning of the bend.

3. Select one of the pardo feathers, clip away the tip at a point where the remaining fibers are all the same length, and trim the butt to remove any web. Stroke back the remaining fibers until there are only five or six left on each side of the feather.

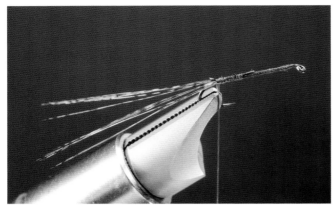

4. Place the tailing feather on top of the hook, and tie it down so that it appears as if you have five or six tailing fibers on each side of the hook. Lash the feather down slightly into the bend of the hook. This will prevent the finished fly from falling over backward.

5. Select two slim pale dun hen hackle feathers, face the shiny sides toward the center, measure for length, and tie them on one hook-gap space behind the eye. Finished wings should be equal in length to the entire hook plus one hook gap.

6. Select two pardo feathers, clip away the butts containing web, and tie them both onto the hook immediately in front of the tailing with the shiny sides up.

7. Palmer the pardo feathers one at a time toward the wing. Leave a little space between each wrap of hackle to accept the next feather. Tie down and clip off the tip.

8. Wrap the second pardo, tie down, and clip off the tip to finish the rear of the body. All the hackle fibers in the rear half of the body should angle slightly to the rear.

9. Trim the butts of the remaining two pardos as described above, and tie them onto the hook shiny side down immediately in front of the last wrap of hackle just finished.

10. Wind the hackles one at a time as described above, making sure there is no gap between the wraps of the rear half and front half of the body.

11. You should have enough hackle to be able to complete a couple of turns in front of the wings with each hackle. All the hackles in the front half of the body should angle slightly forward to prevent the fly from falling over on its face.

This isn't one of the easiest flies you'll ever tie, and it may take several attempts before you get it right. Don't be dismayed. Each year when I replenish my supply of Hovering Crane Flies, I have to tie two or three before I get what I want. Once you get one right, the next few flies will go much easier. Tying with a new material always means you must learn how it wants to be handled.

These are flies that I carry with me only when the hatch is on, because placing them in a regular fly box can cause the long hackle fibers to take a set or get smashed to one side. I figure I need to carry no more than half a dozen of them, so I keep them in a six-compartment box with one fly in each compartment. It's a little bulkier than my other fly boxes but well worth the bother.

Tailing Dry Flies with Coq de Leon

The marvelous advances made by all the hackle growers in recent years are now providing us with hackle quality (in both necks and saddles) we only dreamed about a decade ago. The individual hackle feathers are longer, there are a lot more of them, their quills are finer and stronger, they have more fibers per inch, and they are more consistent in length. Some of the new high-grade saddle hackle feathers will allow you to tie nearly a dozen flies from one feather! Some neck hackle is long enough these days to hackle two or three flies from the same feather. In fact, you almost have to try to tie a poorly hackled fly.

But with all this good news about hackles comes some bad news as well. Where are all those wonderful sides (spades) that we used to use for tailing on our size 16, 14, and 12 dry flies? The genetic trait of longer feathers with shorter hackle fibers has manifested in these feathers as well. You'll be lucky these days to find a good dry-fly neck that has tailing feathers with fibers long enough to tie a size 16 dry fly. You could use guard hair from some small mammals or the hair from deer, elk, or moose, but it isn't always available in the right colors, and much of it is either too soft or breaks off too easily. Microfibetts have become popular with some tiers in recent years, but I don't like the way they wick and hold water. A few tiers I know are raising barnyard-quality roosters just to get some tailing material.

Now comes coq de Leon to our rescue! Whiting Farms has begun raising these wonderful birds and packaging feathers in what are called tailing packs for dry-fly tailing. A package has two or three small pelts that each contain around fifty usable feathers for tailing. Coq de Leon rooster saddles are also available. You'll get a lot more feathers on a saddle, and the size range is from 16 to 12 or larger. The individual feather fibers aren't quite as stiff as those from the humoral tract, but they are still better than anything else we've ever seen or used in the past.

The natural colors of both choices range from an almost silvery white to a golden bronze. I like to get them in the lightest color possible and dye them to the colors I need. The natural silvery white is a good match for many spinner tails, and the various golden to bronze colors work well on some Pale Morning Duns, March Browns, Red Quills, and Rusty Spinners. I dye the silvery white a medium dun and ginger, although the feathers come in a beautiful natural ginger, and I use the bronze as is or dye it brown. I'd guess there is enough tailing material on one saddle to tie a couple hundred dozen flies.

As with any new material used in fly tying, you'll have to learn how it wants to be handled and manipulated as you clip a clump from the quill if you want it to look right after it's tied on the hook. The individual fibers are very hard and stiff, and since there is a slight taper to each fiber, they will migrate out of tip alignment very easily. The more you change grips between hands, the sooner the tips will come out of alignment. You might want to consider a small hair stacker to realign the tips if you're having problems, but be advised that there can be no web at the base of the fibers, as this will prevent the fibers from stacking easily.

Some of the feathers from either the humoral tract or the base of the saddle are no more than 2 or 3 inches long, but they will contain the longest hackle fibers. This means that you should devise some kind of third hand to hold the butt of the feather as you stroke the fibers perpendicular to the quill prior to clipping them off. A big mug of coffee will work (or a stein full of beer!), or you can make a third hand from a tongue depressor and a spring-loaded clothespin. Stroke the fibers just enough to even the tips. This does not always mean at a 90-degree angle to the quill.

Pardo feather stroked to show fiber lengths

Cover the last half of the hook shank with tying thread, clip off enough fibers that you think will look right on the size fly you are tying, measure for length, and tie them onto the hook. This is best done by bringing the tying thread to hang down at the last wrap of thread before the hook bend and placing the clump of tailing fibers against your side of the hook with the butts angling down below the hook shank at a 45-degree angle. Use a very short thread between your bobbin and the hook shank, 1 inch or less. Make a soft loop over both the tailing and the hook, and quickly tighten the thread.

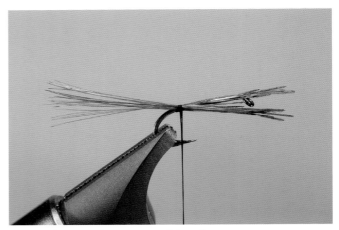

Tailing clump with one turn of thread

Allow the second turn of thread over the tailing butts to roll the butts on top of the hook. Thread torque can be a good thing here. Hold the tips at a 45-degree angle above the hook shank as you do this, and continue wrapping thread over the tailing butts to the shoulder of the body. You will end up with tailing that is slightly cocked upward, much like the naturals.

Completed coq de Leon dry-fly tail

Coq de Leon Hen Backs or Saddles

The coq de Leon hen backs provide a wonderful substitute for partridge hackle on nearly any wet-fly pattern. The individual hackle fibers are quite soft and well marked with mottling that closely resembles the markings on partridge feathers. Coq de Leon hen backs are readily available from most well-stocked fly shops in a variety of both dyed and natural colors. The natural colors range from a light to dark medium dun. I like to purchase the lighter colors and dye them according to my needs, usually light tan, brown, olive, and black.

Natural light and dark coq de Leon hen backs

Dyed coq de Leon hen backs

CHAPTER 12

Translucent Streamers

Ithink many fly tiers and fishers have been sucked into doing a lot of things based on erroneous assumptions. In fact, many of the assumptions we have made about how a fly should look are based on false impressions. There are dozens of examples of this, but I want to deal with one that I feel is very prominent—the erroneous assumption on which we base how we tie streamers.

Look up any article that deals with baitfish or streamers and you will find that the live (or dead) baitfish have been artistically laid out on a piece of driftwood or a large leaf before an artsy picture was taken. The little fish appear very opaque. There will also be photos of imitations that are carbon copies of the natural and equally opaque. It's a classic case of taking something out of its natural environment, photographing it, and believing that is what it should look like when we tie the fly and then fish it in the water. The trouble with that assumption is that the natural baitfish in the water is almost invisible!

I've done a fair amount of snorkeling and am amazed at how translucent all baitfish appear in the water. The first thing I usually see is the eyes, then a thin strip of blue-gray-green along the back, and perhaps a tiny amount of flash along the side of the fish. Nature has designed the prey to be unseen, but she also has designed the predators to detect the prey. The two designs result in a fine balance between predator and prey. If all natural baitfish looked like the streamers we tie, there would be no baitfish or predators!

It's easy to understand, because it's difficult to take photos of baitfish while they are still in the water. And we have dozens of baitfish streamer imitations that were first tied a hundred years or more ago, before the advent of underwater cameras, and have become standard patterns. Traditionalist tiers are hesitant to change anything on an original pattern. I don't believe we are changing anything about a streamer pattern as long as we use the same materials, but less of them to create a sparser fly. This is not always advisable with some patterns that imitate sculpins and muddlers, however, as the bodies of these bottom-dwelling baitfish are quite bulky and very opaque. We also must consider the attractor streamer patterns that have been proven very effective over many decades of use. I'm not convinced that tying attractor streamer patterns sparser would be of any benefit, since they imitate nothing natural. I am convinced, however, that baitfish imitations are far more effective when tied sparser.

Achieving the desired profile of the natural can be a problem when attempting to tie sparse streamers if you don't have the right material. There are a dozen or more manufacturers of synthetic hairlike material whose products work very well for streamer tying. I like to use those that have the most crinkling to their fibers. Wavy bucktail works very well and has some degree of buoyancy to keep the fly upright during the retrieve. Wavy calf-tail hair is good for the smaller bonefish patterns; just be careful how much of it you use. Having said that, I now prefer using arctic fox tail for the wing on any bonefish pattern similar to shrimp patterns such as the Crazy Charlie and Gotcha, because it has a lot more action in the water than the stiffer calf-tail hair, which has been the traditional winging material on many shrimp patterns. Once again, take care not to overdo it. It's easy to use enough winging material to tie three flies. Most shrimp have some degree of translucency as well. The most important trick I learned when using arctic fox tail was to remove a little more than half of the underfur before tying it onto the hook. Too much underfur will choke the action of the longer guard hairs. By the way, arctic fox tail is an excellent substitute for marabou on any fly. Marabou provides lots of action in the water, but it is very fragile; arctic fox tail is surprisingly durable, with the same amount of action as marabou, and is available in all the colors you could possibly need.

A Google search of just half a dozen fly-fishing supply outlets turned up twenty-seven different kinds of synthetic hair or flash material. Add that to the seven to ten common natural materials, and you have a total of almost forty different kinds of materials from which to make streamer wings. It seems as though each month there is yet another new flashier, shinier, more translucent, more flexible, finer must-have material to use for streamer wings. There is a strong temptation to try all of it. I think it's best if you settled on only two or three synthetics, and then used very small amounts—say only one or two strands of carefully selected flash material—blended into a sparse wing of synthetic or natural material. You must remember that the natural baitfish is almost invisible. Keep the wing sparse! You only want to get the fish's attention, not scare it half to death.

Traditional hair-wing streamer with lots of hair and flash material

Sparse hair-wing streamer with little flash material

Gotcha with arctic fox tail wing and antennae

CHAPTER 13

Blue Quill Dun and Parachute

Just about the time I think I have my fly boxes filled with every pattern I'll ever need, I run into a hatch that I can't accurately match. Normally, it doesn't matter if you're fishing an Olive Quill Dun or Parachute when there are blue duns on the water. The trout will usually eat my fly as long as it's the right size and I get a good drag-free drift. Oftentimes it's the old standby Adams that pulls it out for me. But have you ever had one of those days when you just couldn't find the fly the trout wanted? It can happen on hard-fished catch-and-release water. I find that the trout in these waters can get frustratingly selective. It's happened to me too many times in the past couple of years that I happened upon a hatch of Blue Quills but didn't have any.

Now I carry the following Blue Quill Dun pattern in sizes 18 through 12, using dyed wild turkey biots for sizes 14 and 12 and stripped and dyed rooster neck hackle quills for sizes 16 and 18.

Blue Quill Dun

Hook:	Dry-fly sizes, 12–18
Thread:	Danville's gray 6/0, number 31
Tail:	Medium dun spade hackle fibers or dyed coq de Leon pardo or saddle hackle fibers
Body:	For sizes 18 and 16, rooster neck hackle quills stripped and dyed medium dun (two quills for size 16 and one quill for size 18); for sizes 14 and 12, wild turkey biot dyed medium dun, with a dubbed underbody
Wings:	Medium dun hen hackle tips
Hackle:	Medium to dark dun dry-fly hackle

2. Tie on a clump of tailing fibers immediately in front of the tiny thread bump. This will cock the tailing fibers slightly upward. The length of the tailing should be equal to the hook-shank length.

3. For size 18 flies, use one rooster neck hackle quill, stripped and dyed medium dun. Clip off the tip at a point where the remaining diameter is equal to the hook shank, tailing, and thread underbody.

1. Attach tying thread one hook-gap space behind the eye, and wrap to the beginning of the bend. Clip off the tag and take two or three more turns of tying thread over the last turn to create a tiny thread bump.

4. Tie the quill on immediately over the thread starting point, lash it down to the beginning of the bend, and bring the thread forward to the starting point.

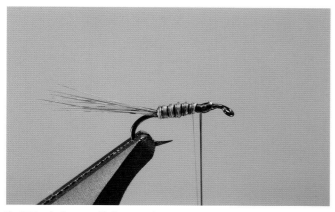

5. Wind the quill forward in tightly nesting wraps to the starting point, tie it off on top of the shank, and clip off the excess. Your quill body is now complete on the size 18 hook.

6. For size 16 flies, use two stripped and dyed quills. Align the quills so that one is twice the diameter of the other. Clip off both tips at a point where their combined width is equal to the hook-eye diameter.

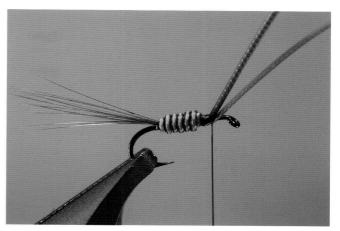

7. Place the quills on top of the hook shank with the thinner quill on the far side and the thicker quill nearest you. Lash them to the rear, bring the thread forward, and wind the quills forward as in tying a size 18 fly. Your size 16 quill body is now complete. *Note:* The thinner quill is only for the underbody and should be completely covered by the thicker one as you wind them forward. You can tie a size 16 fly body with only one quill, but the body silhouette is usually too narrow.

8. Dubbed underbody on size 12 hook: For size 14 and 12 flies, use a wild turkey biot dyed medium dun for the body. Since biots get progressively wider but not thicker as quills do, you'll have to dub an underbody to build up the increasing diameter of the naturals. Dub a body one hook size smaller than the hook you are using. For example, dub a size 14 body on a size 12 hook. Begin the dubbing at the shoulder and taper it to the rear, leaving just enough bare thread for tying in the tip of the biot.

9. Tie on the biot by its tip with only one turn of thread, with the notch at the base of the quill facing the hook eye.

10. Pivot the biot under the single turn of thread until it is at a 90-degree angle to the hook shank. Take three or four turns of thread over the single turn to firmly anchor the tip of the biot. Tying on the biot and pivoting it as described will prevent it from folding on the first turn.

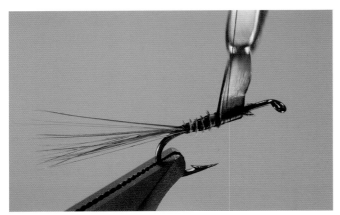

11. Now take a turn of biot followed by a turn of thread over the leading edge of the biot. This will reinforce the biot and prevent the body from coming apart when a trout's tooth hooks into it.

12. Continue winding the biot and the thread until you reach the shoulder of the underbody. Take one more turn of biot and thread in front of the shoulder, clip off the excess biot, and anchor the stub with two or three turns of thread. This completes the biot body.

13. Select a pair of medium dun hen hackle feathers whose tips are as wide as the hook-gap space. Measure them to be as long as the entire hook plus one hook-eye space, and tie them on one hook-eye space in front of the shoulder of the body. This will allow room for two or more turns of hackle behind the wing.

14. Select a medium dun hackle that matches the hook size you are using, and hackle the fly in your favorite manner.

Blue Quill Parachute

Hook:	Dry fly, sizes 18–12
Thread:	Danville's gray 6/0, number 31
Tail:	Same as dun
Wing post:	White turkey T-base segment
Body:	Same as dun
Hackle:	Medium dun one hook size larger

1. Tie on the tail as described in the steps for tying the dun, but make it about two hook-eye spaces longer than the dun tail.

2. Select a white turkey T-base feather with a well-centered quill and very little fringe at the tip.

3. Clip out the center quill to a distance equal to the hook-shank length, and fold fibers back on each side until each of the remaining halves is as wide as the hook-shank length.

4. Fold the two segments into a single clump. Measure the wing-post height to equal the hook-shank length, and tie it onto the hook one and a half hook-eye spaces behind the eye with about seven very firm turns of thread.

5. Lift the butt of the T-base feather, clip it off at an angle, and wrap thread over the clipped-off butt.

6. Bring the thread forward of the post, fold it back, and build up a thread dam in front of the post to stand it erect. Apply a drop of head lacquer to the base of the post, and take several turns of thread around the base to provide a solid area around which to wind the hackle. The wing post is complete.

7. Complete the body of the parachute as per the instructions for tying the dun, but tie the clipped hackle tips immediately behind the wing-post butt. On size 14 and larger flies, where you use a dyed wild turkey biot for the body, begin dubbing an underbody immediately behind the wing-post butt.

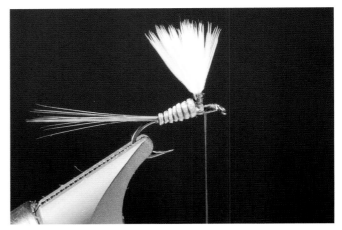

8. Here is the completed quill body.

9. Tie the dubbing on behind the post butt.

10. Here is the completed biot body.

11. Hackle the fly using your favorite method.

CHAPTER 14

Mahogany Quill Spinner

This is another fly that you simply must have when you find mahogany spinners on the water. I've tried the standard Red Quill Spinner, Spent Adams, Olive Quill Spinner, Callibaetis Quill Spinner, and Yellow Quill Spinner in an attempt to fool a few trout when I find the mahogany spinner on the water. I am convinced, after a number of such instances, that trout do indeed perceive color. The last time I tried all these patterns with no success, I finally remembered to net the water to see what the hell the trout were feeding on. There it was, a mahogany spinner, size 14. I had only one in my spinner box that was left over from my Michigan days more than twenty-five years ago. It was a perfect match. It is yet another reason why I carry enough flies in my vest to stock a small fly shop. You can find hatch charts for almost any trout stream in the country that will tell you what should be hatching at any given time of the year, and even the time of day they are likely to occur. The trouble with most of these charts is that they deal only with the major hatches. I guess the authors feel that the minor hatches aren't important enough to take up space in their charts. The failing with that logic is that there are no minor hatches to the trout. Food is food. Or maybe the authors don't know everything. I've yet to meet someone who actually does know everything about trout fishing or aquatic insect hatches. Just about the time I begin to think I know quite a bit, I am completely humbled by something with a brain the size of a pea.

The Mahogany Spinner is a very simple fly that is about three shades darker than a Rusty Spinner or what I tie and call the Red Quill Spinner. Tie at least half a dozen of these spinners in sizes 14 and 16. You never know when you're going to need them.

Mahogany Spinner

Hook:	Your favorite dry-fly hook
Thread:	Danville's black 6/0
Tail:	Brown spade hackle fibers or coq de Leon
Body:	One dark brown rooster hackle quill
Wings:	Light medium dun hen hackle tips
Thorax:	Dark brown dry-fly dubbing

1. Attach the tying thread to the hook about three hook-eye spaces behind the eye, and wind all the way to the beginning of the bend. Take two or three turns of thread over the last turn to create a tiny thread bump.

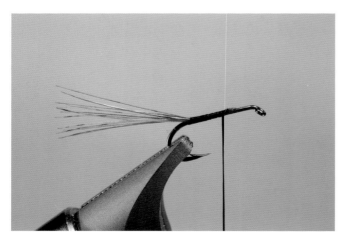

2. Tie in a small clump of tailing fibers immediately in front of the thread bump to cock them up slightly. The length of the tailing fibers should be equal to the entire hook plus one hook-gap space.

3. Lash the tailing fibers up to where you attached the thread, lift the excess butts, and clip them off.

4. Place your materials hand thumbnail under the tailing fibers, and push forward to splay them outward.

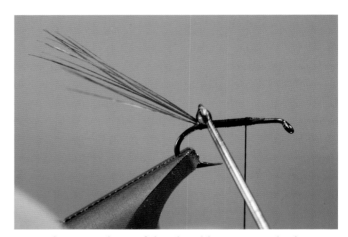

5. Apply a tiny drop of thin head lacquer on the last turn of thread over the tailing. When dry, the tailing fibers will stay in this position, and the lacquer will seal the end of the fly from water absorption.

6. Select one dark brown rooster neck hackle quill, and clip off the tip at a point where the remaining quill tip has a diameter equal to the hook shank, tailing, and thread underbody.

7. Align the clipped tip even with the thread start, lash the quill to the top of the hook to the hook bend, and bring the thread forward to the starting point.

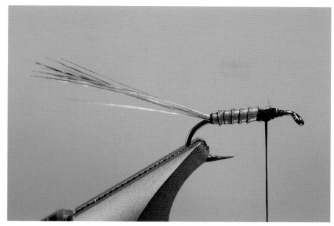

8. Carefully wind the quill forward in tightly nesting wraps to the thread starting point. Tie off the butt on top of the hook, lift it, and cut it away. Cover the clipped butt with tying thread.

9. Select a matched pair of light medium hen hackle tips whose tip width is equal to the hook gap or slightly larger. Measure their length to equal the entire hook plus one hook-eye space.

10. Tie in the hen hackle tips immediately in front of the clipped-off body quill. Separate the tips and press them flat.

11. Figure-eight the wings with thread, and carefully add very thin dubbing to the thread.

12. Carefully build a doughnut-shaped ring of dubbing behind the wings, then build another in front of the wings.

13. Figure-eight wrap more very thin dubbing in front of and behind the two doughnuts to create a thorax and fix the wings in a horizontal position.

14. Creating a thorax on a hen wing spinner in this fashion will provide more stability to the wings and prevent them from folding back in a delta wing style.

15. Whip-finish and apply a tiny drop of head lacquer to the head.

CHAPTER 15

Roy's Biot Emergers

Roy Palm is widely known as the Frying Pan Guru. He's had a fly shop in Basalt, Colorado, the Frying Pan Angler, for as long as I can remember. If you really want to know what's hatching on the Pan, you either stop in and buy a few flies that are hatching that day, or give him a call and he'll gladly tell you what to tie. And if the river is running too high and muddy, he'll tell you that too. I consider Roy one of my best friends, partly because I tied thousands of flies for his shop some years ago and have fished with him many times. He's what I call a "kindred soul."

Roy created a fair number of fly patterns to match both the major hatches and those that were considered by some to be insignificant. There are more than a few of us that believe that no hatch is insignificant if the trout are feeding on it. He created not only the dry-fly and nymph versions of the hatches, but also some marvelously simple emerger patterns he calls Roy's Biot Emergers. The beauty of the Biot Emerger pattern is that when tied in several colors, it perfectly matches a variety of midge and mayfly emerging insects. All you need to do is change the color of the biot. And they can be fished ungreased just under the surface, greased as dry-fly cripples, or with added weight to the tippet to get them down to the depth where the fish are feeding.

The four biot colors are black, dun, olive, and orange. There is no tail or any underbody to build up a silhouette taper. Each pattern color has a tiny ball of medium dun-colored dubbing immediately in front of the shoulder of the body and one or two turns of medium dun hen hackle tied wet-fly style. All are tied with black 6/0 or 8/0 thread on sizes 22 through 16 dry-fly hooks.

The only problem you may have in tying this fly is in finding dun hen necks with feathers whose fibers are short enough to look right on the small hooks. By look right, I mean the hackle tips cannot extend back beyond the hook point. I use my dry-fly hackle gauge to find the right size hackle for each hook size. I suggest seeking out dun hen necks whose hackle tips are rather pointed. These feathers will be longer, with short hackle fibers, and easier to tie on and wind around the hook. Clip off any maraboulike fibers from the base of the feather before tying onto the hook.

The choice of biots is easy: Use either dyed wild turkey or dyed wild goose. In either case, the rough edge of the biot must show and be darker than the wide part.

Tie a bunch of these patterns in each color, because they work anyplace! Spring creeks, rivers, lakes, and ponds all have midge and small mayfly hatches. The colors listed above will match just about every freshwater insect sized 16 and smaller.

Roy's Biot Emergers

1. Debarb the hook, place it in the vise, and attach black 6/0 or 8/0 thread about two hook-eye spaces behind the eye. Wind to the beginning of the bend and clip off the tag.

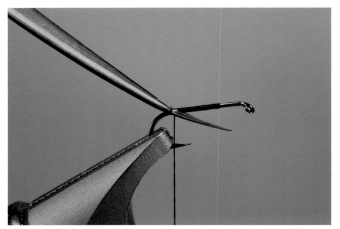

2. Select a biot and attach the tip to the hook, with the notch at the base of the biot facing away from you, with only one turn of thread

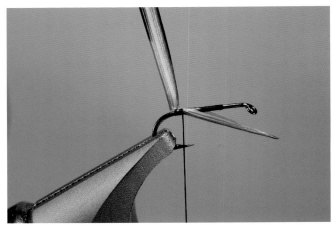

3. Pivot the biot away from you until it is at a 90-degree angle to the hook shank.

4. Take three very firm turns of additional thread over the tip of the biot, and leave the thread hanging at this point.

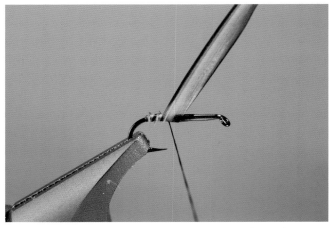

5. Attach the hackle pliers to the butt of the biot and make one turn around the hook, followed by a turn of thread over the leading edge of the biot. This will increase the durability of the biot.

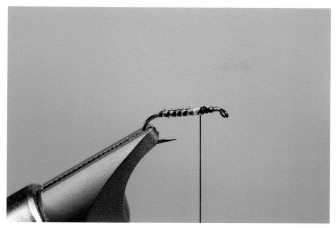

6. Continue winding the biot and the thread forward until you get to a point that is half a hook-gap space behind the eye. Lift the biot butt and clip it off. Cover the clipped-off biot butt with two or three turns of thread.

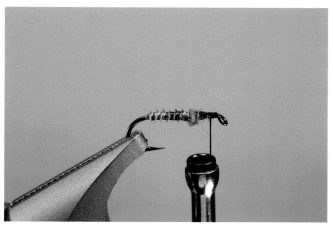

7. Tightly dub a very small ball of dubbing immediately in front of the biot shoulder. I repeat: very small ball of dubbing. The only way to achieve this is to apply just enough dubbing to the tying thread to not quite double its diameter. The diameter of this ball of dubbing should be no larger than twice the diameter of the hook eye.

8. Select a sized hen hackle, strip or clip away all the fluff from the base of the feather, and clip the butt to be no longer than necessary to tie it to the hook.

9. Tie the hen hackle to the hook with the shiny side up and at a slight angle away from you. This will ensure that the hackle feather will go around the hook with its shiny side forward.

10. Take only one or two turns of hackle, being careful that all the fibers lean slightly to the rear.

11. Anchor the tip with just two turns of thread. Lift the tip, clip it off, and whip-finish. Apply a tiny drop of head lacquer to the thread head only.

CHAPTER 16

My Adams

I tied my first Adams dun in 1964, after I moved from Iowa to Michigan and discovered brook trout. Both occurrences changed my life forever. There were lots of brookies and brown trout in the little streams I liked to fish, and the Adams seemed to be one of the few flies I needed. My first attempts were modeled after flies I bought from a local gas and beer store a mile or two from my house. The pointy grizzly hackle tip wings just didn't look right to me, so I began searching through fly-tying books and magazine articles to find what I thought might be the real McCoy. Everything I could find in those days looked pretty much the same as the ones I bought at the gas and beer store—pointy wings and mixed brown and grizzly tailing. I tied them like that for a few years, but I used only brown spade hackle fibers for the tail, because this was a lot easier than stacking mixed tailing fibers. I was never satisfied with the spiky wing appearance, even though the flies caught lots of trout.

After a few years of tying for myself, I began tying for some local shops in Michigan, and word began spreading that I could actually tie flies that other folks would buy. I got a call from John Harder at Orvis asking to see some of my work. I was soon tying Adamses by hundreds of dozens, with plain brown tailing—even though all the pattern recipes for the Adams called for mixed brown and grizzly tailing—and pointy wings. I still wasn't satisfied with the grizzly rooster hackle point wings, so I began saving the points from Hoffman grizzly, which I used in the hackle collar. The orders for more Adamses began to get larger with the increase in the quality of winging material I used. It got to the point where I was buying number two Hoffman grizzly dry-fly necks just to get the winging material. Now, you must understand that this was back in the days when the tips of Henry Hoffman's grizzly dry-fly necks were still rounded. They made the perfect Adams wing. No one ever said anything about the brown tailing.

I happened to go to an estate sale on the banks of the Au Sable River in Michigan, thinking I might be able to pick up some tackle, and purchased a tackle box of old flies. There were hundreds of exquisitely tied old fly patterns, all in individual paper boxes labeled with the pattern name. The one that caught my eye was the box that said, "#14 Adams." Three original Adamses were in that box, and they looked totally different from anything I had seen up to that time. They were tied on long-shank hooks with black thread, a skinny dun body, and golden pheasant tippets for the tail. The grizzly point wings were tied lying flat in a delta wing style, and the hackle was mixed brown and grizzly.

A few years later, I was fishing with Bobby Summers on Michigan's Boardman River. As we stood on an abandoned bridge, looking for trout in a large boiling pool just downstream, he told me the Adams was first fished in that hole. I showed him the pattern I had purchased at the estate sale, and he said, "That's the original pattern. It's changed a little over the years, hasn't it?" I've always wondered who it was that began tying the Adams with upright divided wings and a mixed tail of brown and grizzly hackle fibers.

Back in the early 1980s, after my wife and I moved to Colorado, Bill Keough used to make trips to visit us from his hackle farm, which was then in Iowa (now in Michigan), with a van loaded with feathers. It was the first time I saw grizzly hen capes. They were even better than Hoffman's rooster hackle tips for Adams wings. I began buying them by the dozens and tied even more Adamses for about nine different fly shops.

Adams with pointy wings

Original Adams

My hen wing Adams

All the pattern recipes list muskrat as the body dubbing. What most people don't realize is that there are many shades of gray muskrat underfur. I doubt it makes much difference to the trout what shade of gray is used or if it came from a muskrat. So I settled on medium gray rabbit fur. There was a time when dry-fly dubbing was considered best if it came from an aquatic animal that had lots of waterproofing natural oils. The trouble with that thought these days is that most of the skins you can purchase have been tanned, which removes all the oils and water-repellent capabilities. And most fly fishers these days treat their dry flies with some waterproofing agent, so it doesn't matter what we use for dry-fly dubbing, so long as it's the right color and its mass is lighter than the water it displaces.

My Adams

Hook:	Mustad 94840
Thread:	Danville's black 6/0
Tail:	Brown spade hackle fibers or Coq de Leon
Body:	Medium gray rabbit underfur
Wings:	Grizzly hen neck hackle tips
Hackle:	Mixed brown and grizzly

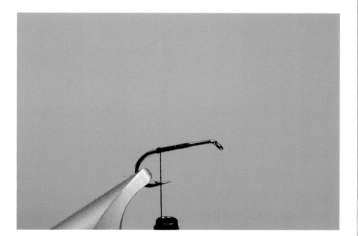

1. Attach the tying thread to the hook one hook-gap space behind the hook eye. This will be the shoulder of the body. Wind the thread to the end of the hook shank, and take two or three turns of thread over the last turn to create a tiny thread bump. This will cock up the tailing fibers slightly.

2. Select a very stiff brown spade hackle or coq de Leon, and clip off an amount of fibers about as wide as the hook-gap space.

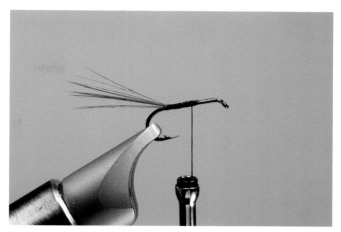

3. Measure the tailing length to equal the length of the entire hook including the eye, and tie on the tailing immediately in front of the tiny thread bump. Lash the tailing fibers up to the thread starting point, lift the butts, and clip them off. Bring the thread back to the end of the hook shank.

4. Begin creating a carrot-shaped body by applying to the tying thread the tiniest tuft of dubbing you can still see. Think of impregnating the thread with dubbing as you do this.

5. Continue to apply slightly larger pinches of dubbing until you think you have enough to make the body. Be careful that the dubbing rope stays very slender but still has some taper to it and is very dense and smooth as possible.

6. Carefully wind the dubbing rope forward to create a slightly tapered body, and stop immediately at the thread starting point.

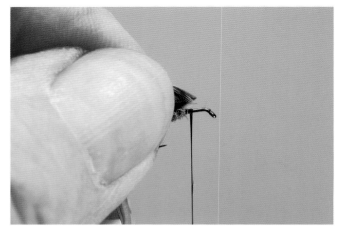

7. Select a pair of well-matched grizzly hen hackle tips whose tip width is equal to the hook-gap space and whose length matches the entire hook plus one hook-eye space.

8. Tie on the wings, with the tips to the rear, slightly in front of the shoulder of the body to save room for two or three turns of hackle. Divide wings into a V shape, and figure-eight with thread to set them.

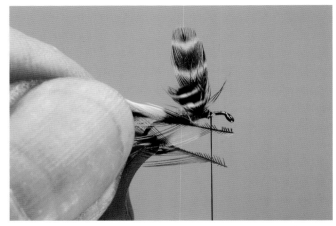

9. The following instructions are for the use of saddle hackles, winding them both at the same time. This will give four total turns of hackle both in front of and behind the wings. Select a brown and grizzly dry-fly hackle whose fiber length is one and a half times the hook-gap space. Trim the butts to allow for tie-down. The sides of the stems that will go around the hook first should be trimmed a little farther back than the length needed for tie-down.

10. Attach the hackle butts in front of the wings. This will cause what's on the hook in front of the wings to be equal in diameter to what's on the hook behind the wings and prevent a cone-shaped hackle collar. Be very certain that the thread hangs down one hook-eye space behind the eye before you begin winding the hackles.

11. Lift the hackles up in front of the wings. Make the first turn of hackles go down in front of the wings and then continue up behind the wings.

12. Take the second turn of hackles immediately behind the first, and then cross forward under the wings for the third turn, which will be in front of the wings.

13. Complete the third turn of hackles in front of the wings, and then take a fourth turn of hackles immediately in front of the third.

14. Stop winding the fourth turn of hackles when they are level with the floor in front of you.

15. Bring the bobbin up behind the hackles until it is parallel to the hackles, and wind both the thread and the hackles around to the far side of the hook, stopping when both are level with the floor on the far side of the hook.

17. Bring the hackles to an upright position and clip off the remainder of the hackles.

16. Hold the hackles in this position and take two more turns of thread over the first turn.

18. Point your scissors directly over the hook eye from the front to clip off any stray hackle fibers.

CHAPTER 17

Saltwater Tips

About twenty years ago, I was tying saltwater flies for two shops in Florida, one in New Hampshire, and one in Vermont. My output amounted to a little over one thousand dozen saltwater flies a year. Tarpon flies, bonefish flies, and billfish flies were the three major categories, with some travally poppers thrown in. Between the saltwater orders and my trout fly orders, I got to the point where I was going to have to either clone myself or give up something. It was an easy choice—I live in trout country.

I learned a few things about how to shorten the time with each fly and how to develop some consistency in their appearance and durability that pleased my accounts and me. One of the biggest time-savers I developed was painting lead barbell eyes. These days, you can purchase them already painted, and some even have little indentations in which to put stick-on pupils. But they'll cost you a little more, and they aren't always the right size or color.

You can easily paint fifty or more barbell eyes at a time by using the following technique:

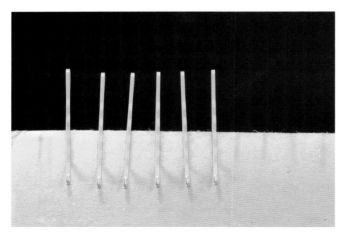

1. Cut an 8-inch-wide strip of stiff corrugated cardboard that is about a foot long.

2. Go to the drugstore and buy a package of bobby pins, the flat kind with little ridges built into one side.

3. Get cans of yellow, white, and red spray enamel (or any needed color).

4. Get bottles of model enamel in black, yellow, and red (or any needed color).

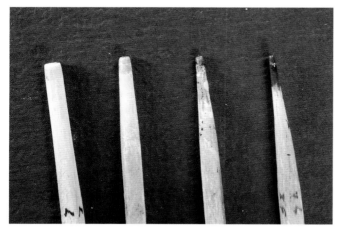

5. Find some regular-size kitchen matches or 1/4-inch-square balsa sticks, and sand one end of each until completely smooth and perfectly round. Carefully scrape off the business ends of the matches until you have something that looks like a screwdriver blade. (This will prevent them from rolling around.) Different-size finish nails will work, but I found their weight to be difficult to control when not in use.

6. Put one barbell lead eye in the looped end of a bobby pin, and slide the flat slide of the bobby pin into one of the hollow cylinders of the corrugated cardboard.

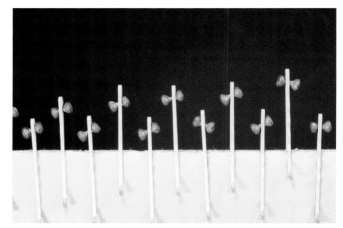
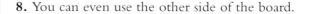

7. Leave a few spaces and do it again . . . as many times as you wish.

8. You can even use the other side of the board.

9. Spray both top and bottom of the barbell eyes with spray enamel.

10. Store the drying board in a vertical position to prevent the paint from drooping, allow the spray to dry completely.

11. Use an appropriate-size matchstick to apply pupils. You can do this while the bobby pins are still in the board if you allowed enough space between eyes.

12. Store the drying board in a vertical position to prevent the paint from drooping as you did in step 9.

13. Allow the painted pupils to dry completely, with the board again kept vertical, and then spray with clear lacquer. This will provide some protection from paint chipping off the eyes.

14. Store the board vertically once more while the lacquer dries. When completely dry, pull the bobby pins from the board. Remove the painted lead eyes to a small storage box, and label the eye size on the side of the box. Save the bobby pins in another box for later use.

I've tied hundreds of dozens of bonefish and tarpon flies whose recipes called for painted lead eyes, and I found this method to be the most efficient. I could be preparing other materials or tying other flies while waiting for the paints to dry.

Some of the patterns I tied called for bead-chain eyes that had to be painted as well. Most of the time, I needed flat or glossy black bead-chain eyes in three different sizes: small, medium (standard key-chain size), and large. Here's what I did:

1. I went to my well-stocked local hardware store and bought six feet of each bead-chain size I needed.

2. When I got the chains home, I cut each one in half with a side cutter.

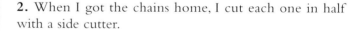

3. I clipped off a 1-foot length of 4-pound-test monofilament, tied a slipknot in each end of the monofilament, and attached a loop to the end of the bead chain.

4. I slipped the other loop of the monofilament over a 1-by-1-inch piece of pine and clamped it to the rail of my deck.

5. Then I sprayed the bead chain with either flat or glossy black spray enamel.

6. The spray paint dried quickly, and then I clipped the bead chain into pairs of eyes and stored them in small boxes labeled with both the color and size of the chain.

Glassy heads can be a problem for both the freshwater and the saltwater tier. A lot of folks use a five-minute epoxy for a quick shiny head. But the problem with this technique is that the heads often turn cloudy after some use in salt water. I think this is because the epoxy never penetrates down to the hook shank through all the thread wraps in the head, and in fact, salt water soaks in from the rear of the head where the winging material was tied on. I have found that if I coat the whip-finished head with a watery thin lacquer, it will soak down to the hook shank, and the head becomes waterproof. Two or three coats of thick lacquer will produce a very glassy head. The only caution in using this method is to take care not to apply too much of the thick lacquer at one time, or it will sag before it can dry. I place the flies with freshly coated heads in Styrofoam blocks to dry for about two hours before applying the second coat. Another two hours of curing time after the second coat, and you're ready to paint on the eyes. You can prevent sagging of both the lacquer coats and the painted eyes by either making a drying wheel, as I described in chapter 8 in my book *Advanced Fly Tying* (Lyons Press, 2001), or purchasing one from your local fly shop or online.

Some bonefish patterns call for glass eyes. These can shatter if your backcast is sloppy and your fly whacks the side of the boat on the forward cast. A good way to make them indestructible is to dip the finished head in clear Dip-It, which you can purchase at most well-stocked hardware stores. Its original intent was to insulate screwdriver handles and pliers from electrical shock. This stuff is bulletproof once it has dried. Simply dip the head and glass eyes of your fly into the container, making sure none of it gets on the wing or hackle collar. Slowly remove the head, and wipe the excess out of the hook eye with the end of a pipe cleaner. Stick the fly in a Styrofoam block to dry. Use Dip-It, head lacquer, or epoxy to seal up the holes in bead-chain eyes as well. They'll get rusty if you don't.

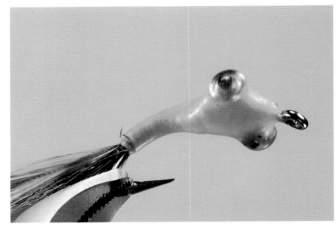

Glass-eyed bonefish fly dipped in Dip-It

Bead-chain bonefish fly with head lacquer or epoxy over eyes

There seem to be some fairly strict style restrictions when tying tarpon flies regarding wing length and whether the wings are tied "wing in" or "wing out." The absolute best feather wing material I have found for tying tarpon flies, including Deceivers, is strung Chinese rooster neck hackle. It's much wider than saddle, maintains its shape better in the water, and has a natural curve in the quill that can be easily matched in pairs or even threes. And it dyes beautifully.

Dyed strung Chinese rooster neck hackle samples

Tarpon flies, wing in and wing out

I etched a wing length template into the top of my fly-tying bench to ensure that each fly I tied appeared to be identical in wing length. Simply line up the tip of a feather to touch the base line, and then cut off the butt at the line indicating the hook size.

Wing template

Clipping feather to length

As you do this, place each feather in a left or right pile. This is important to do, since each feather droops to one side or the other.

Pile of lefts and rights

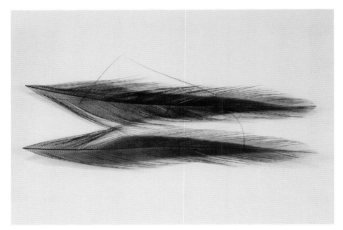

Different tip shapes

Be careful to match the tip shapes when assembling clumps of feathers for left or right wings as well. If the tips are the same shape, there will be less of a tendency for one of the feathers to roll when you tie them onto the hook.

Matched tips

A good method to prevent the feathers from rolling is to lash a short length, about 1/4 inch, of monofilament to the top of the hook just in front of the beginning of the bend. This creates a platform against which you place the trimmed feather butts before tying them onto the hook.

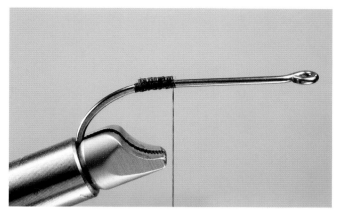

Short length of mono lashed to top of hook near bend

Another method is to carefully squeeze the feather butts flat before tying them on. Be careful with this method that you do not fracture the quill. If you do, it will easily break off.

The only time I ever step-tied flies was when I was tying saltwater flies. I could tie five dozen Deceiver bodies and set them aside as I prepared the wing materials, then add the wing materials and finally paint all the eyes at the same sitting. I thought it saved a lot of time and in fact, it did improve on the proportions of the wing-to-body ratio.

I don't think step-tying standard trout flies is practical. I did it for about half a day over thirty years ago and gave up in frustration over the extra time it took to tie one fly. What I did do to improve my production rate was to get organized: I kept notes on three-by-five inch note cards, created a recipe file, and took photos of the flies I tied. It required some extra time to make the file, but it has become the basis for five books, countless magazine articles, and it remains a quick, detailed reference.

The hints throughout this book should help you become more proficient. You don't need to be a professional tier to be organized.

Index

Supported using public funding by

**ARTS COUNCIL
ENGLAND**

First published in 2018 by the National Theatre
in association with Oberon Books Ltd
Oberon Books Ltd
521 Caledonian Road, London N7 9RH
Tel +44 (0)20 7607 3637
info@oberonbooks.com
www.oberonbooks.com

Book Designer: James Illman

For the National Theatre: National Theatre Publishing

Cover image: The company of *Pericles*
Photograph: James Bellorini

Inside front cover: Vanessa Kirby and Eric Kofi Abrefa in *Julie*
Photograph: Richard H Smith

Inside back cover: HOME Manchester's takeover weekend
of River Stage
Photograph: Cameron Slater

Back cover image: National Theatre, 2017
Photograph: Zefrog / Alamy Stock Photo

PB ISBN: 9781786825780

Printed and bound by
Latimer Trend and Company Ltd., Plymouth, PL6 7PY.

National Theatre
Upper Ground,
South Bank,
London SE1 9PX
www.nationaltheatre.org.uk

Registered Charity No. 224223

Contents

National Theatre

YEARBOOK

2018

OBERON BOOKS

LONDON

A Theatre for Everyone

An introduction from Director Rufus Norris and Executive Director Lisa Burger

This National Theatre never stops; no sooner has one show left than another comes in, and behind that one stretches away a never-ending queue of others, some not even imagined yet. That's how it should be, and how we love it, but now and then it's also good to stop, take a breath, and look back on what we've accomplished. This yearbook is an opportunity to do just that.

It begins, appropriately, with *Beginning*, David Eldridge's touching, understated play about the start of something between two people. And it concludes with the end of a relationship, the world-shaking tragedy of *Antony & Cleopatra*. In between, the NT has brought audiences into the worlds of a puppet who wants to be a real boy (*Pinocchio*), a news anchor who is mad as hell and isn't going to take it any more (*Network*), and a night club proprietress terrified of the moment the party stops (*Absolute Hell*) – to name but a few.

We've had a lot to celebrate this year, including plenty of awards and nominations, but more than that, we're proud of the breadth of the work we've staged, telling more kinds of stories about more kinds of people. Two real milestones for diversity were *The Great Wave,* which featured the first entirely East Asian cast at the NT, and *Nine Night*, which at the time of writing is about to transfer to Trafalgar Studios, making Natasha Gordon the first ever black British female playwright to have a play staged in the West End.

We've also continued to broaden access to our work in any way that we can. In the last 12 months, we have had more shows out on tour than ever before, including *War Horse*, *Hedda Gabler* and schools tours of *The Winter's Tale* and *Macbeth*. NT Live has continued to grow, and now broadcasts to an incredible 2,500 cinemas in 65 countries around the world. And at our South Bank home itself, it's now easier for deaf and hard of hearing people to enjoy our shows through our newly introduced smart caption glasses. Already bookable for some of our productions, from 2019 smart caption glasses will be rolled out for every show, meaning that captions will be available for any performance, not just a few.

Our Learning projects have continued to show children, young people and adults across the country that theatre *is* for them – whether as audiences or as creators, performers, writers, and technicians. In addition to New Views, our writing competition for young people, and Connections, our national theatre festival for young people, 2018 also saw the launch of two new projects. The first, Let's Play, provides specially commissioned scripts with songs and music, along with training for teachers, to support primary schools in putting on their own productions. The second, Public Acts, is a wide-ranging new participatory theatre programme.

The first year of Public Acts culminated in a production of *Pericles* in the Olivier theatre, featuring 123 performers from community groups who had little or no prior experience of theatre, plus a further 99 people from fantastic cameo performance groups. The result was a triumphant celebration of theatre, of community, and of what it feels like to belong. Projects like this are, without question, the most important work this organisation does. It's for that reason that the image for the cover of this yearbook is taken from that production.

We say it a lot, but we can't say it often enough: the National Theatre is for everyone. This yearbook is a record of many exciting theatrical moments, but we hope that it is also a reminder of that fact.

Rufus Norris and Lisa Burger

Opposite page: The company of *Pericles*
Photograph: James Bellorini

Beginning

a new play by **David Eldridge**

Opening Dorfman Theatre, 12 October 2017; Ambassadors Theatre, West End, 15 January 2018
It's the early hours of the morning and Danny's the last straggler at Laura's party. The flat's in a mess. And so are they. One more drink?

Laura **Justine Mitchell**
Danny **Sam Troughton**

West End Understudies
Laura **Zara Plessard**
Danny **Simon Riordan**

Director **Polly Findlay**
Designer **Fly Davis**
Lighting Designer **Jack Knowles**
Sound Designer **Paul Arditti**
Movement **Naomi Said**
Staff Director **Joe Lichtenstein**

Associate Director (West End) **Joe Lichtenstein**
Associate Lighting Designer (West End) **Michael Harpur**
Associate Sound Designer (West End) **Sarah Weltman**

Production Photographer (NT) **Johan Persson**
Production Photographer (West End) **Manuel Harlan**

This page: Justine Mitchell;
Opposite page: Justine Mitchell and Sam Troughton

Photographs: Johan Persson

Network

adapted by **Lee Hall**

based on the **Paddy Chayefsky** film

Opening Lyttelton Theatre, 13 November 2017

Howard Beale, news anchorman, isn't pulling in the viewers. In his final broadcast he unravels live on screen. But when the ratings soar, the network seize on their new found populist prophet, and Howard becomes the biggest thing on TV.

Cast in alphabetical order
Harry Hunter **Charles Babalola**
Technicians **Tobi Bamtefa, Andrew Lewis,**
　Beverley Longhurst, Rebecca Omogbehin
Arthur Jensen **Richard Cordery**
Howard Beale **Bryan Cranston**
Secretary **Isabel Della-Porta**
Diana Christensen **Michelle Dockery**
Director **Ian Drysdale**
Edward Ruddy **Michael Elwyn**
Louise Schumacher **Caroline Faber**
Jack Snowden **Robert Gilbert**
Max Schumacher **Douglas Henshall**
Nelson Chaney **Tom Hodgkins**
Frank Hackett **Tunji Kasim**
Schlesinger **Evan Milton**
Floor Manager **Stuart Nunn**
Continuity Announcer **Patrick Poletti**
ELA Member **Danny Szam**
Production Assistant **Paksie Vernon**

BL!NDMAN [hybrid] Quartet
　Matthew Wright (Musical Director)
　Tom Challenger (Assistant Music Director)
　Kit Downes, Pete Harden, Ed Begley, Alex Bonney,
　Jonas De Roover (Manager)

On Film
News Reporters **Julie Armstrong,**
　Siân Polhill-Thomas and Sid Sagar
News Anchors **Lisa Caruccio Came,**
　Mariam Haque, Mark Inscoe, Paul Lavers
　and Duncan Smith
Verger **Adrian Grove**
Priest **Ian McLarnon**

Director **Ivo van Hove**
Set and Lighting Designer **Jan Versweyveld**
Video Designer **Tal Yarden**
Costume Designer **An D'Huys**
Music and Sound **Eric Sleichim**
Creative Associate **Krystian Lada**
Associate Director **Daniel Raggett**
Associate Set Designer **Paul Atkinson**
Associate Video Designer **Christopher Ash**
Associate Lighting Designer **Marc Williams**
Associate Sound Designer **Alex Twiselton**
Fight Director **Kev McCurdy**
Company Voice Work **Jeannette Nelson**
Dialect Coach **Charmian Hoare**
Staff Director **Jaz Woodcock-Stewart**

Production Photographer **Jan Versweyveld**

Produced in association with Patrick Myles,
David Luff, Ros Povey and Lee Menzies

Presented in association with Dean Stolber

Production supported by Marcia Grand in memory of Richard Grand
and by Kors Le Pere Theatricals LLC.

Opposite page: Stuart Nunn, Charles Babalola and Bryan Cranston
Photograph: Jan Versweyveld

This page:
Top: The company of *Network*; *Bottom:*
Patrick Poletti, Michelle Dockery, Ian Drysdale, Douglas Henshall, Charles Babalola and Paksie Vernon

Opposite page:
Bryan Cranston, Beverley Longhurst, Rebecca Omogbehin and Andrew Lewis

Photographs: Jan Versweyveld

a National Theatre, Fuel and West Yorkshire Playhouse co-production

Barber Shop Chronicles

a new play by **Inua Ellams**

Opening Dorfman Theatre, 20 November 2017

Barber Shop Chronicles had its world premiere at the Dorfman Theatre on 7 June 2017,
followed by a run at West Yorkshire Playhouse from 12 to 29 July 2017

Newsroom, political platform, local hot spot, confession box, preacher-pulpit and football stadium. For generations, African men have gathered in barber shops to discuss the world. These are places where the banter can be barbed and the truth is always telling.

Cast in alphabetical order
Samuel **Fisayo Akinade**
Wallace / Timothy / Mohammed / Tinashe **Hammed Animashaun**
Kwabena / Brian / Fabrice / Olawale **Peter Bankolé**
Musa / Andile / Mensah **Maynard Eziashi**
Tanaka / Fiifi **Simon Manyonda**
Tokunbo / Paul / Simphiwe **Patrice Naiambana**
Emmanuel **Cyril Nri**
Ethan **Kwami Odoom**
Elnathan / Benjamin / Dwain **Sule Rimi**
Kwame / Simon / Wole **Abdul Salis**
Abram / Ohene / Sizwe **David Webber**
Winston / Shoni **Anthony Welsh**

Director **Bijan Sheibani**
Designer **Rae Smith**
Lighting Designer **Jack Knowles**
Movement Director **Aline David**
Sound Designer **Gareth Fry**
Music Director **Michael Henry**
Fight Director **Kev McCurdy**
Staff Director **Stella Odunlami**
Barber Consultant **Peter Atakpo**
Company Voice Work **Charmian Hoare**
Dialect Coach **Hazel Holder**

Production Photographer **Marc Brenner**

Barber Shop Chronicles is co-commissioned by Fuel and the National Theatre.
Development funded by Arts Council England with the support of Fuel, National Theatre, West Yorkshire Playhouse, The Binks Trust, British Council ZA, Òran Mór and A Play, a Pie and a Pint.

Opposite page: Cyril Nri; **Next page:** Members of the company
Photographs: Marc Brenner

Pinocchio

by **Dennis Kelly**
with songs and score from the Walt Disney film by Leigh Harline, Ned Washington and Paul J Smith adapted by **Martin Lowe**

Opening Lyttelton Theatre, 14 December 2017
On a quest to be truly alive, Pinocchio leaves Geppetto's workshop with Jiminy Cricket in tow.
Their electrifying adventure takes them from alpine forests to Pleasure Island to the bottom of the ocean.

Cast in order of appearance
Geppetto **Mark Hadfield**
The Fox **David Langham**
Blue Fairy **Annette McLaughlin**
Pinocchio **Joe Idris-Roberts**
Jiminy Cricket **Audrey Brisson**
Coachman **David Kirkbride**
Lampy **Dawn Sievewright**
Stromboli **Gershwyn Eustache Jnr**
Waxy **Jack North**
Ensemble **Trieve Blackwood-Cambridge, Anabel Kutay,**
　　Clemmie Sveaas, Jack Wolfe
Jiminy Cricket Puppeteer **James Charlton**
Geppetto and Coachman Puppeteers **Stuart Angell,**
　　Michael Taibi, Scarlet Wilderink
Blue Fairy Puppeteers **James Charlton, Rebecca Jayne-Davies,**
　　Sarah Kameela Impey
Stromboli Puppeteers **Rebecca Jayne-Davies, Michael Lin**
Ensemble and Swing **Stephanie Bron, Linford Johnson**

Orchestra
Conductor **Tom Brady**
Keyboard **Amy Shackcloth**
Violin 1 (Leader) / Mandolin **Tom Pigott-Smith**
Violin 2 / Mandolin **Ros Stephen**
Viola **Elizabeth Boyce**
Cello **Dominique Pecheur**
Double Bass **Nicki Davenport**
Guitar / Banjo / Mandolin **Andy Taylor-Vebel**
Drums / Percussion **Mike Parkin**
Woodwind 1: Recorders / Flute / Piccolo **Abigail Burrows**
Woodwind 2: Clarinets / Tenor Recorder **Hannah Lawrance**
Trumpet 1 / Flugel / Piccolo Trumpet **Toby Coles**
Trumpet 2 / Flugel **Martin Evans**
Trombone/ Euphonium **James Adams**
Tuba **Jon Riches**
Harp **Camilla Pay**

Director **John Tiffany**
Set and Costume Designer and Puppet
　　Co-Designer **Bob Crowley**
Music Supervisor and Orchestrations
　　Martin Lowe
Movement Director **Steven Hoggett**
Puppetry Director and Puppet Co-Designer
　　Toby Olié
Lighting Designer **Paule Constable**
Sound Designer **Simon Baker**
Illusions **Jamie Harrison**
Music Director **Tom Brady**
Company Voice Work **Charmian Hoare**
Associate Director **Katy Rudd**
Associate Set Designer **Ros Coombes**
Associate Movement Director **Delphine Gaborit**
Associate Puppetry Director **Sarah Mardel**
Associate Illusion **Chris Fisher**
Staff Director **Maria Crocker**
Assistant Music Director **Amy Shackcloth**

Production Photographer **Manuel Harlan**

By special arrangement with
　　Disney Theatrical Productions

Sponsored by American Express

Opposite page: Joe Idris-Roberts and Mark Hadfield (with Geppetto puppeteers Stuart
Angell, Michael Taibi and Scarlet Wilderink)
Photograph: Manuel Harlan

This page:

Top: Members of the company

Bottom: Audrey Brisson and Joe Idris-Roberts (with Jiminy Cricket puppeteer James Charlton)

Opposite page: Members of the company, including David Kirkbride as the Coachman (with Coachman puppeteers Stuart Angell, Michael Taibi and Scarlet Wilderink)

Photographs: Manuel Harlan

Amadeus

by **Peter Shaffer**

Opening Olivier Theatre, 18 January 2018

Peter Shaffer's iconic play had its premiere at the National Theatre in 1979, before being adapted into an Academy Award-winning film. With live accompaniment by Southbank Sinfonia.

Antonio Salieri **Lucian Msamati**
Wolfgang Amadeus Mozart **Adam Gillen**
Constanze Weber (later Mozart) **Adelle Leonce**
Venticelli **Sarah Amankwah, Ekow Quartey**
Joseph II **Matthew Spencer**
Count Johann Kilian Von Strack **Alexandra Mathie**
Count Franz Orsini-Rosenberg **Hugh Sachs**
Baron Gottfried Van Swieten **Christopher Godwin**
Katherina Cavalieri **Fleur de Bray** (soprano)
Teresa Salieri **Wendy Dawn Thompson**
   (mezzo-soprano)
Salieri's Cook **Peter Willcock** (bass-baritone)
Salieri's Valet **Eamonn Mulhall** (tenor)
Kapellmeister Bonno **Andrew Macbean**
Major-Domo **Everal A Walsh**
Citizens of Vienna
Carleen Ebbs (soprano)
Nicholas Gerard-Martin
Matthew Hargreaves (bass-baritone)
Carla Harrison-Hodge
Michael Lyle
Andrew Macbean
Everal A Walsh
Vocal Understudy **Elizabeth Skinner**

Southbank Sinfonia
Violin I **Ruth Elder** (Leader), **Žanete Uskane**
Violin II **Douglas Harrison, Minsi Yang**
Viola **Jennifer MacCallum, Dan Shilladay**
Cello **Patrick Tapio Johnson,**
   Angélique Lihou
Double Bass **Giuseppe Ciraso Calì**
Flute **Jemma Freestone**
Oboe **Anna Belei, Helen Clinton**
Clarinet **Kimon Parry, Jordi Juan-Perez**
Bassoon **Andrew Watson, Éanna Monaghan**
Horn **Brendan Parravicini, Laetitia Stott**
Trumpet **Sarah Campbell**
Timpani & Percussion **Beth Higham-Edwards**

Director **Michael Longhurst**
Designer **Chloe Lamford**
Music Director & Additional Music
   Simon Slater
Choreographer **Imogen Knight**
Lighting Designer **Jon Clark**
Sound Designer **Paul Arditti**
Company Voice Work **Jeannette Nelson and Rebecca Cuthbertson**
Associate Director **Finn den Hertog**
Associate Sound Designer **Carolyn Downing**
Staff Director **Tom Hughes** (from 12 February)

Production Photographer **Marc Brenner**

This version of *Amadeus* was originally presented as part of the Travelex Season 2017. We are grateful to the executors of the estate of Sir Peter Shaffer for their additional support.

Production supported by the *Amadeus* production syndicate.

Opposite page: Adam Gillen and Lucian Msamati
Photograph: Marc Brenner

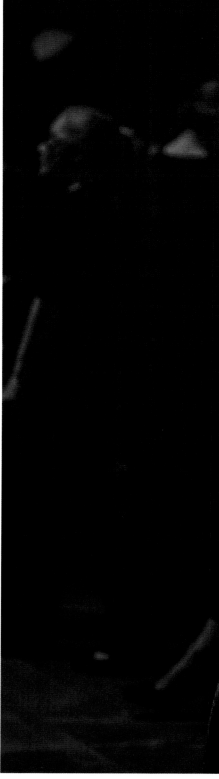

This page:
Lucian Msamati

Opposite page:

Top: Adam Gillen and Christopher Godwin with members of the company

Bottom: Adelle Leonce

Photographs: Marc Brenner

John

by **Annie Baker**

Opening Dorfman Theatre, 24 January 2018

The week after Thanksgiving. A bed and breakfast in Gettysburg, Pennsylvania.
A cheerful host welcomes a young couple struggling to salvage their relationship, while thousands of inanimate objects look on.

Mertis **Marylouise Burke**
Jenny **Anneika Rose**
Elias **Tom Mothersdale**
Genevieve **June Watson**

Marylouise Burke is appearing with the support of UK Equity,
incorporating the Variety Artistes' Federation, pursuant
to an exchange programme between American Equity and UK Equity.

Understudy Mertis/Genevieve **Heather Rome**

Director **James Macdonald**
Designer **Chloe Lamford**
Lighting Designer **Peter Mumford**
Sound Designer **Christopher Shutt**
Dialect Coach **Charmian Hoare**
Staff Director **Rosy Banham**

Production Photographer **Stephen Cummiskey**

World premiere produced by Signature Theatre, New York City
James Houghton, Founding Artistic Director; Erika Mallin, Executive Director

The New American Work Programme is supported by The Harold & Mimi
Steinberg Charitable Trust, Lawton W Fitt & James I McLaren Foundation and Kathleen J Yoh

Opposite page: Tom Mothersdale and Anneika Rose
Photograph: Stephen Cummiskey

This page: *(from clockwise)*
Top right: June Watson;
Bottom right: June Watson and Marylouise Burke;
Bottom left: Anneika Rose and Marylouise Burke;
Top left: Marylouise Burke

Photographs: Stephen Cummiskey

The Winter's Tale

by **William Shakespeare**

in a new version for young audiences by **Justin Audibert and the company**

Opening Dorfman Theatre, 14 February 2018; schools tour 22 January – 9 February 2018

Perdita is a brave, intelligent and much-loved girl, but something is not quite right in her world.
Join her on a journey through magic and mayhem as she uncovers her story – the girl who was once lost and then found.
The perfect introduction to Shakespeare for younger audiences. Warning: watch out for pursuing bears!

Cast in order of speaking

Perdita / Mamillius **Gabby Wong**
Polixenes **Adrian Richards**
Leontes **Nana Amoo-Gottfried**
Hermione / Young Shepherd **Tamara Camacho**
Camilla **Shazia Nicholls**
Antigonus / Old Shepherd **Johndeep More**
The Officer / Florizel **Kenton Thomas**
Paulina **Stephanie Levi-John**

Director **Justin Audibert**
Designer **Lucy Sierra**
Composer & Musical Director **Jonathan Girling**
Lighting Designer **Paul Knott**
Puppet Designer **Sam Wyer**
Sound Designer **Mike Winship**
Movement Director **Lucy Cullingford**
Company Voice Work **Rebecca Cuthbertson**
Staff Director **Sophie Moniram**

Production Photographer **Ellie Kurttz**

Partner for Learning Bank of America Merrill Lynch

Supported by The Mohn Westlake Foundation, The Ingram Trust,
Archie Sherman Charitable Trust, Behrens Foundation,
Cleopatra Trust, The Ernest Cook Trust, Jill and David Leuw,
Mulberry Trust, Newcomen Collett Foundation,
The Royal Victoria Hall Foundation, St Olave's Foundation Fund,
and The Topinambour Trust.

This page: Tamara Camacho;
Opposite page: The company, including Gabby Wong and Stephanie Levi-John
Photographs: Ellie Kurttz

Macbeth

by **William Shakespeare**

Opening Olivier Theatre, 6 March 2018

The ruined aftermath of a bloody civil war. Ruthlessly fighting to survive, the Macbeths are propelled towards the crown by forces of elemental darkness.

Cast in alphabetical order
Gentlewoman **Nadia Albina**
Doctor **Michael Balogun**
Duncan **Stephen Boxer**
Lady Macbeth **Anne-Marie Duff**
Porter **Trevor Fox**
Siward / Murderer **Andrew Frame**
Banquo **Kevin Harvey**
Witch / Boy **Hannah Hutch**
Lennox **Nicholas Karimi**
Macbeth **Rory Kinnear**
Murderer **Joshua Lacey**
Rosse **Penny Layden**
Witch **Anna-Maria Nabirye**
Lady Macduff **Amaka Okafor**
Macduff **Patrick O'Kane**
Ensemble **Hauk Pattison**
Murderer **Alana Ramsey**
Witch **Beatrice Scirocchi**
Fleance **Rakhee Sharma**
Malcolm **Parth Thakerar**

Musicians
Bass Clarinet / New Wind Instruments **Sarah Homer**
French Horn / New Wind Instruments **Laetitia Stott**

Director **Rufus Norris**
Set Designer **Rae Smith**
Costume Designer **Moritz Junge**
Lighting Designer **James Farncombe**
Music **Orlando Gough and Marc Tritschler**
Sound Designer **Paul Arditti**
Movement Director **Imogen Knight**
Fight Directors **Kev McCurdy and Jeremy Barlow**
Pole Captain **Hauk Pattison**
Instrument Maker, Sonic Bricolage **Simon Allen**
Company Voice Work **Jeannette Nelson**
Associate Designer **Aaron Marsden**
Staff Director **Liz Stevenson**

Production Photographer **Brinkhoff/Mögenburg**

Production sponsored by Travelex

Opposite page: Anne-Marie Duff and Rory Kinnear
Photograph: Brinkhoff/Mögenburg

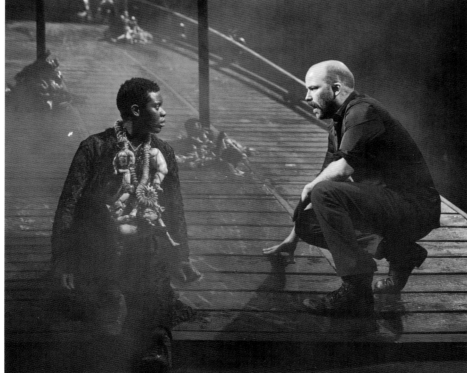

This page:
Top: Rory Kinnear;
Bottom: Anna-Maria
Nabirye and
Rory Kinnear

Opposite page:
Anne-Marie Duff,
Michael Balogun and
Nadia Albina

Photographs:
Brinkhoff/Mögenburg

a co-production with the Tricycle Theatre

The Great Wave

a new play by **Francis Turnly**

Opening Dorfman Theatre, 19 March 2018

On a Japanese beach, teenage sisters Hanako and Reiko are caught up in a storm. Reiko survives while Hanako is lost to the sea. Their mother, however, can't shake the feeling that her missing daughter is still alive, and soon family tragedy takes on a global political dimension.

Cast in order of speaking

Etsuko **Rosalind Chao**
Hanako **Kirsty Rider**
Reiko **Kae Alexander**
Tetsuo **Leo Wan**
Takeshi / Jiro **David Yip**
Official **Kwong Loke**
Jung Sun **Tuyen Do**
Kum-Chol **Vincent Lai**
Hana **Frances Mayli McCann**
Soldier One **Chike Chan**
Soldier Two **Tuyen Do**

Rosalind Chao is appearing with the support of UK Equity incorporating the Variety Artistes' Federation, pursuant to an exchange programme between American Equity and UK Equity

Director **Indhu Rubasingham**
Designer **Tom Piper**
Video Designer **Luke Halls**
Lighting Designer **Oliver Fenwick**
Music **David Shrubsole**
Sound Designer **Alexander Caplen**
Movement Director **Polly Bennett**
Fight Director **Kev McCurdy**
Company Voice Work **Charmian Hoare**
Staff Director **Jennifer Bakst**

Production Photographer **Mark Douet**

Thanks to The Great Britain Sasakawa Foundation.

The Channel 4 Playwrights' Scheme celebrates and supports emerging British writing talent. The initiative (formerly the Pearson Playwrights' Scheme) awards five bursaries a year to new theatre writers and has been supported by Channel 4 since 2013. Four bursaries are supported by Channel 4 and the fifth by The Peggy Ramsay Foundation. Francis Turnly wrote *The Great Wave* while on attachment at Tricycle Theatre, as part of the scheme. It won the Catherine Johnson Best Play Award in 2016.

Opposite page: Rosalind Chao
Photograph: Mark Douet

This page:
Left: Kwong Loke and Kirsty Rider;
Below: Kirsty Rider and Kae Alexander

Opposite page:
Top: Members of the company;
Bottom right: Kirsty Rider and Rosalind Chao

Photographs: Mark Douet

Absolute Hell

by **Rodney Ackland**

Opening Lyttelton Theatre, 25 April 2018

Bomb-blasted London. A Soho den in the hangover from World War II, where members drink into the darkness, night after night. Lying, fighting and seducing, these lost souls and bruised lovers struggle from the rubble of war towards an unknown future.

Cast in order of speaking

Christine Foskett **Kate Fleetwood**
Doris **Stephanie Jacob**
Cook **Fiz Marcus**
Butch **Aaron Heffernan**
Julia Shillitoe **Patricia England**
Hugh Marriner **Charles Edwards**
Siegfried Shrager **Danny Webb**
Elizabeth Collier **Sinéad Matthews**
Mrs Marriner **Joanna David**
Michael Crowley **Lloyd Hutchinson**
Sam Mitchum **Martins Imhangbe**
Maurice Hussey **Jonathan Slinger**
Lettice Willis (The Treacle Queen) **Liza Sadovy**
Cyril Clatworthy **Esh Alladi**
Bill **Anita Reynolds**
R B Monody **Jenny Galloway**
Madge **Eileen Walsh**
Douglas Eden **John Sackville**
Non-Member **Jonathan Coote**
Nigel Childs **Prasanna Puwanarajah**
Mrs Pratt **Carole Dance**
PC Molson **Ashley Byam**
DI Roach **Simon Hepworth**
Fifi **Rachel Dale**
Club Members **Esh Alladi, Elizabeth Andrewartha, Ashley Byam, Jonathan Coote, Carole Dance, Frazer Hadfield, Simon Hepworth, Fiz Marcus, Connor Mills, Anita Reynolds, John Sackville, Liza Sadovy, Jade Yourell**
Typists **Jessica Brindle, Holly Hudson, Laura-Joy Pieters**

Director **Joe Hill-Gibbins**
Set Designer **Lizzie Clachan**
Costume Designer **Nicky Gillibrand**
Lighting Designer **Jon Clark**
Associate Director and Movement **Jenny Ogilvie**
Sound Designer **Paul Arditti**
Music Director **Harvey Brough**
Company Voice Work **Jeannette Nelson**
Dialect Coach **Charmian Hoare**
Staff Director **Ali Pidsley**

Production Photographer **Johan Persson**

Opposite page: Kate Fleetwood
Photograph: Johan Persson

This page:
Above: Members of the company including
Rachel Dale and Lloyd Hutchinson;
Below right: Kate Fleetwood and Aaron
Heffernan; *Right:* Charles Edward

Opposite page:
Top: Sinéad Matthews;
Below: Members of the company

Photographs: Johan Persson

Nine Night

a new play by **Natasha Gordon**

World premiere Dorfman Theatre, 30 April 2018

Gloria is gravely sick. When her time comes, the celebration begins; the traditional Jamaican Nine Night Wake. But for Gloria's children and grandchildren, marking her death with a party that lasts over a week is a test. Nine nights or music, food, sharing stories – and an endless parade of mourners.

Cast in alphabetical order

Robert **Oliver Alvin-Wilson**
Lorraine **Franc Ashman**
Uncle Vince **Ricky Fearon**
Trudy **Michelle Greenidge**
Sophie **Hattie Ladbury**
Anita **Rebekah Murrell**
Aunt Maggie **Cecilia Noble**

Director **Roy Alexander Weise**
Designer **Rajha Shakiry**
Lighting Designer **Paule Constable**
Sound Designer **George Dennis**
Movement Director **Shelley Maxwell**
Fight Director **Bret Yount**
Company Voice Work **Rebecca Cuthbertson**
Dialect Coach **Hazel Holder**
Staff Director **Jade Lewis**
Assistant to the Movement Director **Sarita Piotrowski**

Production Photographer **Helen Murray**

This page:
Top: Oliver Alvin-Wilson and Ricky Fearon;
Bottom: Franc Ashman, Rebekah Murrell, Oliver Alvin-Wilson, Ricky Fearon and Cecilia Noble

Opposite page:
Top: Hattie Ladbury and Franc Ashman;
Bottom: Franc Ashman, Ricky Fearon, Cecilia Noble, Michelle Greenidge and Rebekah Murrell

Photographs: Helen Murray

Translations

by **Brian Friel**

Opening Olivier Theatre, 30 May 2018

Owen, the prodigal son, returns to rural Donegal from Dublin. With him are two British army officers. Their ambition is to create a map of the area, replacing the Gaelic names with English. It is an administrative act with radical consequences. Brian Friel's modern classic is a powerful account of nationhood, which sees the turbulent relationship between England and Ireland play out in one quiet community.

Cast in order of speaking

Manus **Seamus O'Hara**
Jimmy Jack Cassie **Dermot Crowley**
Sarah **Michelle Fox**
Maire **Judith Roddy**
Doalty **Laurence Kinlan**
Bridget **Aoife Duffin**
Hugh **Ciarán Hinds**
Owen **Colin Morgan**
Captain Lancey **Rufus Wright**
Lieutenant Yolland **Adetomiwa Edun**
Other parts played by members of the company

Understudies
Manus/Doalty/Owen **Steve Cash**
Lieutenant Yolland **Adam Collier**
Jimmy Jack Cassie/Hugh **Aidan Dooley**
Captain Lancey **Nigel Fairs**
Sarah/Maire/Bridget **Niamh McGowan**

Musicians
MD and Guitars **Dario Rossetti-Bonell**
Double Bass **Nicki Davenport**
Viola **Anna Cooper**
Percussion **Stephen Hiscock**

Director **Ian Rickson**
Designer **Rae Smith**
Lighting Designer **Neil Austin**
Music **Stephen Warbeck**
Sound Designer **Ian Dickinson**
Movement **Anna Morrissey**
Company Voice Work **Charmian Hoare and Jeannette Nelson**
Dialect Coach **Majella Hurley**
Staff Director **Shane Dempsey**
Associate Sound Designer **Alexander Caplen**

Production Photographer **Catherine Ashmore**

Production sponsored by Travelex

Opposite page: Seamus O'Hara, Dermot Crowley and Michelle Fox
Photograph: Catherine Ashmore

This page:
Top: Judith Roddy and Dermot Crowley;
Bottom: Adetomiwa Edun,
Colin Morgan and Seamus O'Hara
Opposite page: Ciarán Hinds

Photographs: Catherine Ashmore

Julie

by **Polly Stenham**, after Strindberg

Opening Lyttelton Theatre, 7 June 2018

Wild and newly single, Julie throws a late-night party. In the kitchen, Jean and Kristina clean up as the celebration heaves above them. Crossing the threshold, Julie initiates a power game with Jean. It descends into a savage fight for survival. Fuelled by social division, Strindberg's masterpiece remains shocking and fiercely relevant in this new version by Polly Stenham.

Cast in order of speaking

Jean **Eric Kofi Abrefa**
Kristina **Thalissa Teixeira**
Julie **Vanessa Kirby**

Partygoers
Temitope Ajose-Cutting
El Anthony
Thomasin Gülgeç
Francesca Knight
Dak Mashava
Michela Meazza
Ana Beatriz Meireles
Ashley Morgan-Davies
Rebecca Omogbehin
Yuyu Rau
Petra Söör

Supernumeraries
Subika Anwar-Khan
Steven Bush
Holly Rose Hawgood
Tom Kelsey
Olivia Leat
Tucker McDougall
Josefine Reich
Elliott Rogers
Sophie Spreadbury

Understudies
Jean **El Anthony**
Kristina **Rebecca Omogbehin**
Julie **Francesca Knight**

Director **Carrie Cracknell**
Designer **Tom Scutt**
Lighting Designer **Guy Hoare**
Movement Director **Ann Yee**
Music **Stuart Earl**
Sound Designer **Christopher Shutt**
Fight Director **Owain Gwynn**
Illusions **Chris Fisher**
Video Designer **Mogzi Bromley-Morgans**
Company Voice Work **Jeannette Nelson**
Staff Director **Jo Tyabji**
Associate Movement Director **Michela Meazza**

Production Photographer **Richard H Smith**

Production sponsored by Travelex

Opposite page: Eric Kofi Abrefa and Vanessa Kirby
Photograph: Richard H Smith

This page:
Top: Eric Kofi Abrefa;
Bottom: Members of the company
including Francesca Knight,
Vanessa Kirby and Petra Söör

Opposite page:
Top: Thalissa Teixeira and Eric Kofi Abrefa;
Bottom: Vanessa Kirby

Photograph: Richard H Smith

a co-production with the Orange Tree Theatre

An Octoroon

by **Branden Jacobs-Jenkins**

Opening Dorfman Theatre, 14 June 2018

This production of *An Octoroon* had its European premiere at the Orange Tree Theatre on 18 May 2017.

Branden Jacobs-Jenkins' extraordinary play comes to the National Theatre after a sold-out run at the Orange Tree Theatre. In 1859, white Irish playwright Dion Boucicault writes a hit play about America. Today, a black American playwright attempts to do the same.

BJJ / George / M'Closky **Ken Nwosu**
Playwright / Wahnotee / Lafouche **Kevin Trainor**
Assistant / Pete / Paul **Alistair Toovey**
Minnie **Vivian Oparah**
Dido **Emmanuella Cole**
Grace / Br'er Rabbit **Cassie Clare**
Dora **Celeste Dodwell**
Zoe **Iola Evans**

Cellist **Kwêsi Edman**

Director **Ned Bennett**
Designer **Georgia Lowe**
Lighting Designer **Elliot Griggs**
Movement Director **Ivan Blackstock**
Music **Theo Vidgen**
Sound Designer **George Dennis**
Puppetry **Jimmy Grimes**
Music Director **Michael Henry**
Fight Director **Kev McCurdy**
Company Voice Work **Rebecca Cuthbertson**
Dialect Coach **Mary Howland**
Staff Director **Steven Kavuma**

Production Photographer **Helen Murray**

Sponsored by Delta Air Lines

An Octoroon had its World Premiere at Soho Rep, NYC.
Sarah Benson, Artistic Director; Cynthia Flowers, Executive Director

Subsequently produced by Theatre for a New Audience.
Jeffrey Horowitz, Founding Artistic Director; Henry Christensen III, Chairman;
Dorothy Ryan, Managing Director at the Polonsky Shakespeare Center, Brooklyn, NY in 2015

The New American Work Programme is supported by the Harold and Mimi Steinberg Charitable Trust, Lawton W Fitt and James I McLaren Foundation, and Kathleen J Yoh.

Opposite page: Ken Nwosu and Alistair Toovey
Photograph: Helen Murray

This page:
Top: Vivian Oparah and Celeste Dodwell;
Bottom: Ken Nwosu

Opposite page:
Top: Ken Nwosu;
Bottom: Emmanuella Cole and Alistair Toovey

Photographs: Helen Murray

Connections 2018

Opening National Theatre Connections Festival, 26 – 30 June 2018, Dorfman Theatre

Each year the National Theatre commissions ten new plays for young people to perform, bringing together some of the UK's most exciting writers with the theatre-makers of tomorrow. Over 270 school and youth theatre companies from across the UK took part in Connections 2018, and 5,200 young people had the opportunity to stage a production at one of our 28 Partner Theatres. Ten companies were invited to perform at the National Theatre's Connections Festival.

[BLANK]
by Alice Birch
A National Theatre/Clean Break co-commission
Performed by See&Eye Theatre, Performing Arts students from City and Islington College, London

The Changing Room
by Chris Bush
Performed by students studying for Performing Arts diplomas at Cornwall College, St Austell

Want
by Barney Norris
Performed by students from St Brendan's Sixth Form College, based in Bristol

The Sweetness of a Sting
by Chinonyerem Odimba
Performed by students aged 13–14 years from Haggerston School in Hackney, London

The Ceasefire Babies
by Fiona Doyle
Performed by Yew Tree Youth Theatre from Wakefield, West Yorkshire

These Bridges
by Phoebe Eclair-Powell
Performed by an integrated youth theatre group, including young people with additional needs, from Chichester Festival Theatre

The Free 9
by In-Sook Chappell
Performed by TRANSMISSION youth theatre group from Jackson's Lane in Highgate, London

The Blue Electric Wind
by Brad Birch
Performed by Collison, a youth theatre group for young people across Central Scotland

When They Go Low
by Natalie Mitchell
Performed by students from CAPA College, a specialist arts college in Wakefield, Yorkshire

Dungeness
by Chris Thompson
Performed by PACE Youth Theatre, based in Paisley, Scotland

Connections 2018 plays commissioned by Tom Lyons

Partner for Learning Bank of America Merrill Lynch

Connections is supported by The Mohn Westlake Foundation, The Buffini Chao Foundation, Andrew Lloyd Webber Foundation, Delta Air Lines, Jacqueline and Richard Worswick, Peter Cundill Foundation, Mactaggart Third Fund, The EBM Charitable Trust, Samantha and Richard Campbell-Breeden, The Garvey Family Trust, Susan Miller and Byron Grote, Anthony P Skyrme, The Broughton Family Charitable Trust, The Derrill Allatt Foundation, Hays Travel Foundation, Faithorn Farrell Timms and supporters of the Connections appeal.

Partner Theatres
01 Aberystwyth Arts Centre
02 The Albany, London
03 artsdepot, London
04 The Bush Theatre, London
05 Cast, Doncaster
06 Chichester Festival Theatre
07 Derby Theatre
08 Eden Court, Inverness
09 The Garage, Norwich
10 HOME, Manchester
11 The Lowry, Salford
12 Lyric Hammersmith, London
13 Lyric Theatre, Belfast
14 Marlowe Theatre, Canterbury
15 North Wall Theatre, Oxford
16 Northern Stage, Newcastle
17 Norwich Playhouse
18 Queen's Theatre, Hornchurch
19 Royal & Derngate, Northampton
20 Sheffield Theatres
21 Sherman Theatre, Cardiff
22 Soho Theatre, London
23 Theatre Royal, Bath
24 Theatre Royal, Plymouth
25 Theatre Royal Stratford East, London
26 Traverse Theatre, Edinburgh
27 Warwick Arts Centre
28 West Yorkshire Playhouse, Leeds

Opposite page: *Top: These Bridges* performed by Chichester Festival Youth Theatre; *Bottom: [BLANK]* performed by See&Eye Theatre
Photographs: Richard H Smith

a co-production with Neal Street Productions

The Lehman Trilogy

by **Stefano Massini**; adapted by **Ben Power**

Opening Lyttelton Theatre, 12 July 2018

On a cold September morning in 1844 a young man from Bavaria stands on a New York dockside. Dreaming of a new life in the new world, he is joined by his two brothers and an American epic begins. 163 years later, the firm they establish – Lehman Brothers – spectacularly collapses into bankruptcy, and triggers the largest financial crisis in history.

Cast in order of speaking

Henry Lehman **Simon Russell Beale**
Emanuel Lehman **Ben Miles**
Mayer Lehman **Adam Godley**

Janitor **Dominik Tiefenthaler**
Piano **Candida Caldicot**

Understudies
Henry Lehman **Leighton Pugh**
Emanuel Lehman **Dominik Tiefenthaler**
Mayer Lehman **Will Harrison-Wallace**
Piano **Yshani Perinpanayagam**

Supernumeraries
Alexander Ballinger
Gary Bland
Stephen Cheriton
John Davitt
Murat Erkek
Chris Fung
Neil Gardner
Laura Glover
Robin Hellier
Saskia Marland
Robert Moore
Derek Oppong
Spencer Lee Osborne
Greg Page
Drew Paterson
Nick Potts
Kate Sketchley
Mark Steere

Director **Sam Mendes**
Set Designer **Es Devlin**
Costume Designer **Katrina Lindsay**
Video Designer **Luke Halls**
Lighting Designer **Jon Clark**
Composer and Sound Designer **Nick Powell**
Music Director and Piano **Candida Caldicot**
Movement **Polly Bennett**
Associate Director **Zoé Ford**
Associate Lighting Designer **Ben Pickersgill**
Technical Sound Associate **Dominic Bilkey**
Company Voice Work **Charmian Hoare**

Production Photographer **Mark Douet**

Sponsored by The Wall Street Journal and Financial News

Opposite page: Simon Russell Beale, Ben Miles and Adam Godley
Photograph: Mark Douet

This page: Simon Russell Beale
Opposite page: Ben Miles, Adam Godley and Simon Russell Beale
Photographs: Mark Douet

New Views 2018

New Views is the National Theatre's annual playwriting competition for 14 to 19-year-olds. It gives young people across the country the chance to write a play – and one student each year sees their play produced at the National Theatre. This year, students from 74 schools submitted over 300 plays. There were 101 longlisted scripts, ten shortlisted scripts and one final winner.

Winning Play: **If We Were Older**
by **Alice Schofield**
CAPA College, Wakefield

At first glance, Daisy and Maggie don't seem to have much in common. Daisy is 18, inquisitive, brave and looking hopefully to the future. Maggie is in her 70s, wistful and full of regret. When they meet on a busy tube train, they clash.

Growing up decades apart, but tied together by a shared love of women, their experience of life is more similar than either of them realise.

Opening 11–13 July, Dorfman Theatre

Cast
Phoebe Frances Brown
Katie Buchholz
Michelle Fox
Gaby French
Shalisha James-Davis
Valerie Lilley
Lily Nichol
Sabrina Sandhu

Director **Rachel Lincoln**
Designer **Sadeysa Greenaway-Bailey**
Lighting **Paul Knott**
Movement **Coral Messam**
Sound **Jack Lord**

Shortlisted plays:

£39
by **Rachel Lane**
The Becket School, Nottingham

It's More Than Okay Levi
by **Robert Samuel Lazarus**
Haberdashers' Aske's Boys' School, Hertfordshire

Ashes to Ashes, Oolong to Assam
by **Sol Alberman**
Camden School for Girls, London

Blue is a Boy's Colour
by **Star Gaze**
Camden School for Girls, London

A Broken Usra
by **Mohamed Elsandel**
Woolwich Polytechnic School, London

Cleanse
by **George Jacques**
Whitgift School, London

See You, Space Cowboy
by **Dara Hughes**
The Skinners' School, Kent

Holiday Destination
by **Miriam Warm**
Allerton High School, Leeds

No Sympathy for the Devil
by **Luke Berridge**
Wallington County High School, London

Readings of shortlisted plays:
12–13 July, Dorfman Theatre

Production Photographer **Ludovic des Cognets**

New Views is supported by The Mohn Westlake Foundation, Old Possum's Practical Trust, Chapman Charitable Trust, Golsoncott Foundation and The Steel Charitable Trust

Partner for Learning: Bank of America Merrill Lynch

Opposite page: Lily Nichol, Gaby French and Shalisha James-Davis in *If We Were Older*
Photograph: Ludovic des Cognets

Exit the King

by **Eugène Ionesco**; in a new version by **Patrick Marber**

Opening Olivier Theatre, 25 July 2018

Somewhere in Europe the kingdom is disintegrating. It's the last day of King Bérenger's life. Queen Marguerite is preparing for the end and Queen Marie is in denial. The King is 400 years old and dying, but he's clinging on for dear life…

Cast in order of speaking

The Guard **Derek Griffiths**
Queen Marguerite **Indira Varma**
Juliette **Debra Gillett**
Queen Marie **Amy Morgan**
The Doctor **Adrian Scarborough**
King Bérenger **Rhys Ifans**

Musician **Sarah Campbell**

Understudies
The Guard/The Doctor **Jeremy Bennett**
Queen Marguerite **Emma Thornett**
Juliette **Jane MacFarlane**
Queen Marie **Natalie Law**
King Bérenger **Russell Wilcox**

Director **Patrick Marber**
Designer **Anthony Ward**
Lighting Designer **Hugh Vanstone**
Music and Sound **Adam Cork**
Movement **Emily-Jane Boyle**
Company Voice Work **Jeannette Nelson**
Staff Director **Anna Girvan**

Production Photographer **Simon Annand**

Production sponsored by Travelex

This page:
Above: Derek Griffiths and Indira Varma; *Right:* Rhys Ifans and Adrian Scarborough

Opposite page:
Top: Derek Griffiths; *Bottom:* Debra Gillett and Rhys Ifans

Photographs: Simon Annand

Home, I'm Darling

a new play by **Laura Wade**

Opening Dorfman Theatre, 31 July 2018

Home, I'm Darling had its world premiere at Theatr Clwyd, 3 July 2018

Every couple needs a little fantasy to keep their marriage sparkling. But behind the gingham curtains, things start to unravel, and being a domestic goddess is not as easy as it seems. This new comedy is about one woman's quest to be the perfect 1950s housewife.

Cast in order of speaking

Judy **Katherine Parkinson**
Johnny **Richard Harrington**
Fran **Kathryn Drysdale**
Sylvia **Sian Thomas**
Alex **Sara Gregory**
Marcus **Barnaby Kay**

Director **Tamara Harvey**
Designer **Anna Fleischle**
Lighting Designer **Lucy Carter**
Sound Designer **Tom Gibbons**
Choreographer **Charlotte Broom**
Staff Director **Hannah Noone**

Associate Designer **Ruth Hall**
Associate Lighting Designer **Sean Gleason**
Associate Sound Designer **Harry Johnson**
Assistant Choreographer **Christopher Akrill**

Production Photographer **Manuel Harlan**

Sponsored by Delta Air Lines

Opposite page: Katherine Parkinson
Photograph: Manuel Harlan

This page:

Top: Kathryn Drysdale and Barnaby Kay

Bottom: Barnaby Kay and Katherine Parkinson

Opposite page:
Katherine Parkinson and Richard Harrington

Photographs:
Manuel Harlan

a Wardrobe Ensemble and Wardrobe Theatre Production

The Star Seekers

by **the Wardrobe Ensemble**

Opening Dorfman Theatre, 8 August 2018

Star Seekers Alph, Betty and Gammo need your help to save their space station, collect all the orbs and delve into the great unanswered question of the universe: what do astronauts really have for tea? This interactive family show allows audiences to take the steering wheel and shape the story, and the actors improvise the rest. Discover strange worlds, create solar system soundscapes, decide the noises of the aliens and even fire asteroids through space!

Cast

Betty **Jesse Meadows**
Gammo, Composer and Sound Designer **Jack Drewry**
Alph **Ben Vardy**

Director **Helena Middleton**
Designers **Nicola Holter and Katie Sykes**
Company Producer **Hannah Smith**
Younger Years Producer **Emily Greenslade**

Production Photographer **Ellie Kurttz**

Sponsored by Delta Air Lines

This page: Jesse Meadows, Ben Vardy and Jack Drewry
Opposite page: Jesse Meadows, Jack Drewry and Ben Vardy
Photographs: Ellie Kurttz

River Stage Festival

River Stage showcases an incredible mix of free, outdoor, live entertainment every summer at the National Theatre. Across five weekends between July and August, visitors can see an eclectic range of events; from raves, drag acts and cabaret, to striking dance and theatre performances. In 2018, the River Stage saw four of the UK's leading arts companies take over the stage, with The Glory, HOME Manchester, Sadler's Wells and nonclassical creating a spectacle on the South Bank, culminating in a closing weekend curated by the National Theatre.

This year's takeovers:

13–15 July: **The Glory**
Featuring:
Un-Royal Variety
Virgin Xtravaganzah
Lipsync1000!
Radical Fairy Party
Lorraine Bowen
John Sizzle's Disney Hour
The Baby Lame Poop Show
Big Gay Songbook
Sex Shells
Sodom & Begorah Irish Party!
Jonny Woo's 'Liza with a Z'
John Sizzle's 'Iconic Cabaret!'
Apoca-Lipstick Anthems Party!
Drag Life Drawing
Timberlina
The Sound of Musicals

20–22 July: **HOME, Manchester**
Featuring:
Bourgeois & Maurice
Dave Haslam
Olivia Laing
Mufti Games
Mighty Heart Theatre
The Beat Chics
Monkeywood Theatre
Manchester International Roots Orchestra
DJ Paulette
Young Identity
Juba do Leão

27–29 July: **Sadler's Wells**
Featuring:
Breakin' Convention
Bright Dawn Yoga
Lindy Hop Open Workshop
Rambert2
Step Change Studios
Vidya Patel & Shammi Pithia
Dotdotdot Dance
The Dance WE Made
Company of Elders
Ceilidh Liberation Front

3–5 August: **nonclassical**
Featuring:
Nick Luscombe
Klavikon
Tom Richards
DOLLYman
Cecilia Bignall
Sarah Dacey
Peter Gregson
Cello Multitracks
DJ Mr Switch
Eleanor Ward
Tre Voci
Imprint

10–12 August: **National Theatre**
Featuring:
Extraordinary Bodies
Concrete Disco
SESSION
Empire Sounds
The Wardrobe Ensemble
Mrs H and the Sing-along Band
Pericles Band
Zilla Night feat. Blondezilla & D'Vo
Ball Room Dance Band
Shirt Tail Stompers
NT Live of *Follies*

Photographs by **Cameron Slater**
Additional photographs by **Stephanie Lodge**

Sponsored by Delta, Hertz, Stage Sound Services Ltd and Strand & VariLite

Opposite page: Extraordinary Bodies, part of the National Theatre's weekend
Photograph: Cameron Slater

Clockwise from top left: SESSION, part of the National Theatre's weekend; DJ Paulette, part of HOME, Manchester's weekend; Rambert2, part of Sadler's Wells' weekend; Le Gateau Chocolat performing in The Sound of Musicals, part of The Glory's weekend; Cecilia Bignall, Colin Alexander and Gregor Riddell perform Cello Multitracks, part of nonclassical's weekend

Photographs: Cameron Slater

Pericles

by **William Shakespeare**; in a version by **Chris Bush**; with music by **Jim Fortune**

Opening Olivier Theatre, 26–28 August 2018

Prince Pericles has everything but understands little. When a reckless act threatens his safety, he must flee his home and take to the sea. Reliant on the whims of the fates and the kindness of strangers, Pericles is driven from shore to shore.

Pericles launched Public Acts, our new nationwide initiative to create extraordinary acts of theatre and community. The programme aims to build sustained partnerships with communities and theatres across the UK, through which we will create ambitious new works of participatory theatre.

Cast in order of appearance (*Members of Actors' Equity)

Prologue Chorus **Blessing Anosike, Ayo Dapo-Ayodele, Michael Maloney, Rehma Nangendo**
Pericles **Ashley Zhangazha***
Pericles' Retinue **Omar Alfrouh, Rosalind Stevens**
Helicanus **Les Devonshire**
Selene **Marjorie Agwang**
Antiochus **Deevan Nembhard**
Guards **Quinton Birdas, Nic Morris**
Cleon **Garry Robson***
Dionyza **Blossom Sandra Cole**
Thaisa **Naana Agyei-Ampadu***
Simonida **Ayesha Dharker***
Tarsus Advisors **Josephine Appiah, Olaide Folorunsho, Geoff Street, Chris Wertheim**
Tarsus Entertainers **Angela Barroso, Lisa Brown, Fabienne Crocket, Gary Green, Consilia Kgatitsoe, Cleopatra Ralph, Gamila Street, Alyscia Waheed**
Tarsus Messenger **Shungu Govera**
Fishers **Rachel Adesanya, Agapi Alexandre, Cass Alexandre, Mequannt Assefa, Ayo Dapo-Ayodele, Claudia Dattoli, Neil Dowden, Rachel Harris, Priya Kaur, Tony Khan, Chaimaa Ormazabal, Connor O'Toole, Philip Owusu, Victoria Sanders, Sanketa Shetty, Erma Simon**
Maids **Diana Malunga Yese, Juno Amina Koroma, Clio Motunrayo Oyetunji, Metis Nadege Rene, Rhea Hannah Miles, Corin Michelle Frans-Dapaah**
Suitors **David Buttigieg, Paris Easton, Edris Olive, Mieko Wertheim**
Cerimon **Sophie Mathieson-Medrano**
Tellus **Kevin Williams**
Child Marina **Helen Adesanya**
Child Philoten **Maleah Lisath-Gregory**
Tween Marina **Kareena Thind**

Tween Philoten **Rachel Adesanya**
Delegates **Sue Agyakwa, Luthfun Nessa Choudhury, Haider Saleem, Catherine Tollington**
Marina **Audrey Brisson***
Philoten **Olivia Small**
Teens **Shelley Bockor, Mwila Chilufya, Noor Kalumba, Zeba Easmin Koli, Dean Makin, Laura Mulligan**
Pirate Queen **Gemma Vilanou**
Pirates **Sharon J Bidecant, Louise Duguid, Aaron Edo-Osagie, Michelle Ezeuko, Percy Hammond, Precious A Jacob, Paul Lepper, Sandra Nakigagga, Deevan Nembhard, Kenny Nkwabilo, Tugba Tirpan**
Pander **Humfrey Mwanje**
Bawd **Tallulah-Grace Wheeler**
Boult **Kevin Harvey***
Citizens of Tyre, Tarsus, Pentapolis and Mytilene **Louie Alexandre, Collette Anderson, Sandra Anlin, Douglas Bannister, Mamataj Begum, Lilian Bennett, Tomah Brown, Alfred Camilleri, Maria Camilleri, Carol Anne Cooper, Annabelle Ferary, Rosy Govera, Gaura-Hari Harbal, Sade Hewitt-Ibru, Tish Inglis, Kay Pall Kaur, Beena Khan, Munira Lazarus, Jane Lebbie, Demsey Legrand, Jamie Liddle, Thulani Maadza, Tristan McDermot, Lindsay McDougall, Elizabeth Martindale, Stephanie Nunn, Gemma Nurudeen, Candida Owusu, Charlotte Peach, Thomas Proszowski, Alya Rashid, Layla Shirreh, Derek Sibbering, Rowanne Simpson, Manjit Kaur Singh, Hollie Smith, Saroj Vadher, Ketrin Vardiashvili, Denise Vilanou, Eveline Williams, Simon Wright, Yasin Zayan-Rashid**
Musicians **Fred Thomas** (Piano / Bass / Guitar) **Ross Hughes** (Saxophone / Bass Clarinet / Keys) **Nathaniel Keen** (Guitar / Bass) **Nick Pynn** (Strings) **Magnus Mehta** (Percussion)

Cameo Performance Groups

Ascension Eagles **Suraya Monteiro, Kamdi Chukwuma, Tia Foley, Reanne Rubio, Kennedy Olaniran, Zara Bahay, Darja Rustamova, Macy-Leigh Bromley, Marshe Kupara, Janelle Basilio, Alexandra Martelly, Mailyn Caperros-Lyug, Saskia Olaniran, Taya Melius, Stephanie Hedges, Maddie Parrish, Jada Small**

Faithworks Gospel Choir **Marcia McPherson, Rita Quarry, Nicole Miller, Cecile Smith, Rodrick Gray, Neville Johnson, Sharon Johnson, Jola Olaide, Nnenna Anyanwu, Francesca Nwanosike, Elodie Unia, Rebekah Spencer, Lorna Haywood, Jodie Ricketts, Frances Heath, Grace Adelakan, Mary Reid, Junie Joseph, Nkechi Anyanwu Jaja**

The Bhavan Centre Drummers **Dhanraj Persaud, Soumyaraj Das, Nerrusan Sivaharan**

The London Bulgarian Choir **Dessislava Stefanova** (soloist), **Alex Gibson, Alison Conway, Catriona Langmuir, Charles Ryan, Claire Coxhill, Deanna Benedict, Diana Koleva, Diana Tsekova, Eleanor Roberts, Emily Wasp, Geoff Burton, Ginka Mastoridis, Helen Brice, Iris Luppa, Jana Haragalova, John Moore, Jordan Gogov, Kasia Sommerfeld, Lora Kaleva, Lucy Gibson, Margaret Luck, Polina Hidzheva, Polly Hunt, Radoslava Leseva, Ron Fielder, Steven East, Ulrike Speyer, Valentina Parvanova**

The Youthsayers Ska Band **Elijah Clarke, Mina Hernandez David, Lani Hernandez David, Nicolas Gomez, Josie Hopwood, Khush Quiney, Thabo Witter**

Manifest Nation **T Damien Anyasi, Marcella Shkrelli, Esme Bacalla Hayes, Macaulay Nicholson, Angelika Napierala, Zihong Mok, Kadeem Akinyemi, Dyal Schuember, Tru Peñate, Sepehr Dashtipour**

The Archetype Dance Team **Mike Igbins, Jesse Erhabor, Amona Kadiku, Shirley Ahura, Jadesola Adesola, Dorine Mwesiga, Asha Verma, Temica Thompson, Dee Gyasi-Sonukan, Imani Clovis, Pav Rai, Amadu Mansaray, Jessica Owens**

Director **Emily Lim**
Designer **Fly Davis**
Choreographer **Robby Graham**
Lighting Designer **Paule Constable**
Sound Designer **Paul Arditti**
Music Director **Tarek Merchant**
Company Voice Work **Hazel Holder**
Assistant Director **Gethin Evans**
Rehearsal Director **Jon Beney**

Dramaturg **Nina Steiger**
Associate Lighting Designer **Rob Casey**
Music Associate **Marc Tritschler**
Public Acts Associates **James Blakey, Gethin Evans, Corinne Meredith, Philip Morris, Brian Mullin** and **Diana Vucane** (Assistant)
Dance Captains **Arran Green, Kane Husbands, Laura Meaton and Corinne Meredith**
Fight Director **Kev McCurdy**

Community Partners **Body & Soul, Bromley by Bow Centre, Coram, DABD, The Faith & Belief Forum, Havering Asian Social Welfare Association (HASWA), Open Age and Thames Reach**
Theatre Partner **Queen's Theatre Hornchurch**

Production Photographer **James Bellorini**

Public Acts is supported by Arts Council England's Strategic Touring Fund, Bloomberg Philanthropies, Hertz, The Sackler Trust and Garfield Weston Foundation.

The National Theatre's Partner for Learning is Bank of America Merrill Lynch

Public Acts is inspired by Public Works, the Public Theater's ground-breaking programme of participatory theatre in New York, by the National Theatre's own experience of creating *we're here because we're here* and by the visionary participatory work of other theatres across the UK over the past decades.

Opposite page: Ashley Zhangazha (right of image) with members of the *Pericles* company
Previous page: Kevin Harvey and Audrey Brisson (centre) with members of the *Pericles* company
Photographs: James Bellorini

The Prisoner

Text by **Peter Brook** and **Marie-Hélène Estienne**

Opening Dorfman Theatre, 17 September 2018

The Prisoner had its world premiere at Théâtre des Bouffes du Nord, 6 March 2018

Somewhere in the world, a man sits alone outside a prison. Who is he, and why is he there? Is it a choice or a punishment?

Cast in alphabetical order

Mavuso **Hiran Abeysekera**
Ezekiel **Hervé Goffings**
Man / Guard **Omar Silva**
Nadia / Guard 1 **Kalieaswari Srinivasan**
Visitor / Guard 2 **Donald Sumpter**

Co-Director **Peter Brook**
Co-Director **Marie-Hélène Estienne**
Lighting Designer **Philippe Vialatte**
Stage Elements **David Violi**

Technical Manager **Philippe Vialatte**
Company Manager **Adeline Vicart**
Costume Assistant **Alice François**

Production Photographer **Ryan Buchanan**

A co-production with C.I.C.T / Théâtre des Bouffes du Nord;
The Grotowski Institute; Ruhrfestspiele Recklinghausen;
Yale Repertory Theatre; Theatre For A New Audience – New York

Sponsored by Delta Air Lines

This page: *Bottom left:* Hervé Goffings and Kalieaswari Srinivasan; *Bottom right:* Donald Sumpter and Hiran Abeysekera
Opposite page: Hiran Abeysekera and Omar Silva
Photographs: Ryan Buchanan

Antony & Cleopatra

by **William Shakespeare**

Opening Olivier Theatre, 26 September 2018

Caesar and his assassins are dead. General Mark Antony now rules alongside his fellow defenders of Rome. But at the fringes of a war-torn empire the Egyptian Queen Cleopatra and Mark Antony have fallen fiercely in love. In a tragic fight between devotion and duty, obsession becomes a catalyst for war. Politics and passion are violently intertwined in Shakespeare's gripping tale of power.

Cast in order of speaking

Caesar **Tunji Kasim**
Agrippa **Katy Stephens**
Cleopatra **Sophie Okonedo**
Antony **Ralph Fiennes**
Eros **Fisayo Akinade**
Charmian **Gloria Obianyo**
Iras **Georgia Landers**
Soothsayer **Hiba Elchikhe**
Enobarbus **Tim McMullan**
Proculeius **Ben Wiggins**
Sicyon Official **Shazia Nicholls**
Lepidus **Nicholas Le Prevost**
Thidias **Sam Woolf**
Pompey **Sargon Yelda**
Menas **Gerald Gyimah**
Varrius **Waleed Hammad**
Euphronius **Nick Sampson**
Octavia **Hannah Morrish**
Canidius **Alan Turkington**
Scarus **Alexander Cobb**
Ventidius **Henry Everett**

Musicians
Music Director / Percussion **Magnus Mehta**
Percussion **Joley Cragg**
Cello **Kwêsi Edman**
Woodwind **Sarah Manship**
Guitar / Oud **Arngeir Hauksson**

Supernumeraries
Samuel Arnold
Catherine Deevy

Director **Simon Godwin**
Set Designer **Hildegard Bechtler**
Costume Designer **Evie Gurney**
Lighting Designer **Tim Lutkin**
Music **Michael Bruce**
Movement Directors **Jonathan Goddard and Shelley Maxwell**
Sound Designer **Christopher Shutt**
Video Designer **Luke Halls**
Music Director **Magnus Mehta**
Fight Director **Kev McCurdy**
Associate Director **Emily Burns**
Associate Costume Designer **Laura Hunt**
Company Voice Work **Jeannette Nelson**

Production Photographer **Johan Persson**

Official Hotel Partner Edwardian Hotels

Production supported by Areté Foundation / Betsy & Ed Cohen, Mary M. Miner, and supporters of the *Antony & Cleopatra* production appeal

Opposite page: Members of the company including Katy Stephens, Tunji Kasim and Sophie Okonedo
Photograph: Johan Persson

Clockwise from top left: Tim McMullan and Nicholas Le Prevost; *Middle:* Ralph Fiennes; *Top right:* Sophie Okonedo; *Bottom right:* Sophie Okonedo and Ralph Fiennes; *Bottom left:* Tunji Kasim and Hannah Morrish

Photographs: Johan Persson

Angels in America
A Gay Fantasia on National Themes

by **Tony Kushner**

Opening Neil Simon Theatre, 24 March 2018

America in the mid-1980s. In the midst of the AIDS crisis and a conservative Reagan administration, New Yorkers grapple with life and death, love and sex, heaven and hell.

Cast in order of appearance

Millennium Approaches

Rabbi Isidor Chemelwitz / Hannah Pitt / Ethel Rosenberg / Henry **Susan Brown**

Roy M Cohn / Prior 2 **Nathan Lane**

Joseph Pitt / Prior 1 / The Eskimo **Lee Pace**

Harper Pitt / Martin Heller **Denise Gough**

Mr Lies / Belize **Nathan Stewart-Jarrett**

Louis Ironson **James McArdle**

Prior Walter / The Man in the Park **Andrew Garfield**

Emily / Sister Ella Chapter / A Homeless Woman / The Angel **Amanda Lawrence** / **Beth Malone**

Angel Shadows **Rowan Ian Seamus Magee**, **Matty Oaks**, **Jane Pfitsch**, **Ron Todorowski**, **Silvia Vrskova**, **Lucy York**

Perestroika

Aleksii Antedilluvianovich Prelapsarianov / Hannah Pitt / Henry / Ethel Rosenberg / The Angel Asiatica **Susan Brown**

Louis Ironson / The Angel Australia **James McArdle**

Joseph Pitt / The Angel Europa **Lee Pace**

Mr Lies / Belize / The Angel Oceania **Nathan Stewart-Jarrett**

Harper Pitt / The Angel Africanii **Denise Gough**

Prior Walter **Andrew Garfield**

The Angel / Mormon Mother **Amanda Lawrence** / **Beth Malone**

Roy M Cohn / The Angel Antarctica **Nathan Lane**

Angel Shadows **Rowan Ian Seamus Magee**, **Matty Oaks**, **Genesis Oliver**, **Jane Pfitsch**, **Lee Aaron Rosen**, **Ron Todorowski**, **Silvia Vrskova**, **Lucy York**

Directed by **Marianne Elliott**

Scenic Design **Ian MacNeil**

Costume Design **Nicky Gillibrand**

Lighting Design **Paule Constable**

Puppetry Director & Movement **Finn Caldwell**

Music by **Adrian Sutton**

Sound Design **Ian Dickinson** for Autograph

Movement Consultant **Steven Hoggett**

Hair/Wig & Makeup Design **Rick Caroto**

Original Movement **Robby Graham**

Puppet Design **Finn Caldwell** and **Nick Barnes**

Illusions **Chris Fisher**

Casting **Jim Carnahan, C.S.A.** and **Charlotte Bevan**

Associate Directors **Gina Rattan** (US) and **Miranda Cromwell** (UK)

Movement Associate **Patrick McCollum**

Design Adaptation **Edward Pierce**

Production Stage Manager **Kristen Harris**

Associate Producers **Franki De La Vega**, **Red Awning/Nicole Kastrinos**

Advertising & Marketing **Serino Coyne**

Press Representative **DKC/O&M**

Production Management **Aurora Productions**

General Management **Bespoke Theatricals**

Support for the work of the National Theatre in The United States is led by the American Associates of the National Theatre.

The producers wish to express their appreciation to Theatre Development Fund for its support of this production.

The producers wish to thank the Public Theater for its support of *Angels in America.*

Susan Brown, Amanda Lawrence, James McArdle and Nathan Stewart-Jarrett are appearing with the support of Actors' Equity Association pursuant to an exchange program between American Equity and UK Equity. Denise Gough is appearing with the support of Actors' Equity Association.

This page: Amanda Lawrence
Photograph by Helen Maybanks

Originally produced on Broadway by Jujamcyn Theaters and Mark Taper Forum/Gordon Davidson, with Margo Lion, Susan Quint Gallin, Jon B. Platt, The Baruch-Frankel-Viertel Group and Frederick Zollo in association with Herb Alpert.

Presented by Tim Levy for NT America; Jordan Roth; Rufus Norris & Lisa Burger for the National Theatre; Elliott & Harper Productions; Kash Bennett for NT Productions; Aged In Wood; The Baruch-Viertel-Routh-Frankel Group; Jane Bergère; Adam Blanshay Productions; Catwenjam Productions; Jean Doumanian; Gilad-Rogowsky; Gold-Ross Productions; The John Gore Organization; Grove Entertainment; Harris Rubin Productions; Hornosmoellenberg; Brian & Dayna Lee; Benjamin Lowy; Stephanie P. McClelland; David Mirvish; Mark Pigott KBE; KStJ; Jon B. Platt; E. Price-Ld Ent; Daryl Roth; Catherine Schreiber; Barbara Whitman; Jujamcyn Theaters; The Nederlander Organization; The Shubert Organization

At the Young Vic and in the West End; a National Theatre and Young Vic co-production with Good Chance Theatre

The Jungle

by **Joe Murphy** and **Joe Robertson**

Opening at the Young Vic Theatre, 15 December 2017; at the Playhouse Theatre in the West End, 5 July 2018

Meet the hopeful, resilient residents of The Jungle – just across the Channel, right on our doorstep. Join the residents over fresh-baked naan and sweet milky chai at the Afghan Café, and experience the intense, moving and uplifting encounters between refugees from many different countries and the volunteers who arrive from the UK.

Cast at the Young Vic Theatre
Henri/Yasin **Raphael Acloque**
Norullah **Mohammad Amiri**
Maz **Elham Elsas**
Boxer **Trevor Fox**
Omid **Moein Ghobsheh**
Derek **Michael Gould**
Safi **Ammar Haj Ahmad**
Mohammed **Ansu Kabia**
Yohannes **Bruk Kumelay**
Sam **Alex Lawther**
Paula **Jo McInnes**
Okot **John Pfumojena**
Beth **Rachel Redford**
Ali **Rachid Sabitri**
Salar **Ben Turner**
Helene **Nahel Tzegai**
Omar **Mohamed Sarrar**
Amal **Aliya Ali** / **Alyssa De Souza**

Cast at the Playhouse Theatre
Mahmoud **Tiran Aakel**
Norullah **Mohammad Amiri**
Boxer **Gerard Carey** / **Trevor Fox**
Henri/French Police Officer/CRS **Alexander Devrient**
Maz **Elham Elsas**
Omid **Moein Ghobsheh**
Safi **Ammar Haj Ahmad**
Tarek **Cherno Jagne**
Angela **Kiki Kendrick**
Sam **Alex Lawther** / **Freddie Meredith**
Paula **Jo McInnes**
Omar **Mohamed Sarrar**
Rahel **Sara Mokonen**
Hamid **Yasin Moradi**
Mohammed **Jonathan Nyati**
Okot **John Pfumojena**

Beth **Rachel Redford**
Derek **Dominic Rowan**
Ali **Rachid Sabitri**
Yasin **Eric Sirakian**
Salar **Ben Turner**
Helene **Nahel Tzegai**
Amal **Aliya Ali** / **Alyssa De Souza** / **Lara Alpay** / **Erin Rushidi**

Directors **Stephen Daldry** and **Justin Martin**
Set Designer **Miriam Buether**
Costume Designer **Catherine Kodicek**
Lighting Designer **Jon Clark**
Sound Designer **Paul Arditti**
Musical Director / Composer **John Pfumojena**
Casting **Julia Horan CDG**

Production supported by Glenn and Phyllida Earle and Clive and Sally Sherling

Presented in the West End by Sonia Friedman Productions and Tom Kirdahy, Hunter Arnold in association with Elizabeth Dewberry & Ali Ahmet Kocabiyik, Paula Marie Black, Michael Desantis, Tulchin Bartner Productions, 1001 Nights Productions, Rupert Gavin, Brenda Leff, Stephanie P. McClelland, Richard Winkler, Jane Cee & Glenn Redbord

Opposite page: Ben Turner and Moein Ghobsheh
Photograph: Marc Brenner

Consent

a play by **Nina Raine**

Opening Harold Pinter Theatre, 29 May 2018; world premiere at the National's Dorfman Theatre, 4 April 2017

Why is Justice blind? Is she impartial? Or is she blinkered? Friends take opposing briefs in a contentious legal case. The key witness is a woman whose life seems a world away from theirs. At home, their own lives begin to unravel as every version of the truth is challenged.

Cast in alphabetical order
Kitty **Claudie Blakley**
Edward **Stephen Campbell Moore**
Rachel **Sian Clifford**
Gayle/Laura **Heather Craney**
Zara **Clare Foster**
Tim **Lee Ingleby**
Jake **Adam James**

Understudies
Rachel/Gayle/Laura **Emma Carter**
Tim/Jake **Pete Collis**
Edward **David Mildon**
Kitty/Zara **Katie Wimpenny**

Director **Roger Michell**
Set **Hildegard Bechtler**
Costume **Dinah Collin**
Lighting **Rick Fisher**
Music **Kate Whitley**
Sound **John Leonard and Sarah Weltman**
Casting **Amy Ball CDG**
Associate Director **Titas Halder**

Special thanks to: Oliver Bagby, Hallie Davies, Freya Hounslow, Shay Hurley, Lexi Roach, Hunter Greaves, Hamish Oliver- Howar, Jacob Lawrence Hodges, Georgina Cousins and Ethan James Fletcher for playing baby Leo.

Consent was originally commissioned by Out of Joint and co-produced by the National Theatre and Out of Joint.

Presented by the National Theatre and Sonia Friedman Productions in Association with William Archer, Rupert Gavin, Gavin Kalin Productions, Adam Blanshay Productions/Eilene Davidson, Scott M. Delman, AK, Monkstown Associates, Tulchin Bartner Productions

Opposite page: Claudie Blakley, Sian Clifford and Adam James
Photograph: Johan Persson

In the West End

The National Theatre, Ambassador Theatre Group, Gavin Kalin Productions, Glass Half Full Productions, Fiery Dragons/Olympus Theatricals and Neil Laidlaw present

The Lincoln Center Theater production of

Oslo

a new play by **J. T. Rogers**

Opening Harold Pinter Theatre, 11 October 2017; *Oslo* had its premiere at Lincoln Center Theater, New York, on 16 June 2016;
Oslo opened at the National's Lyttelton Theatre on 15 September 2017

In 1993, in front of the world's press, the leaders of Israel and Palestine shook hands on the lawn of the White House. Few watching would have guessed that the negotiations leading up to this iconic moment started secretly in a castle in the middle of a forest outside Oslo. *Oslo* tells the true story of two maverick Norwegian diplomats who coordinated top secret talks and inspired seemingly impossible friendships. Their quiet heroics led to the ground-breaking Oslo Peace Accords.

Cast in alphabetical order

Marianne Heiberg / Toril Grandal **Geraldine Alexander**
Uri Savir **Philip Arditti**
Jan Egeland / Ron Pundak **Thomas Arnold**
Hassan Asfour **Nabil Elouahabi**
German Wife / Swedish Hostess / Understudy Mona Juul,
    Marianne Heiberg and Toril Grandal **Karoline Gable**
Shimon Peres / Yair Hirschfeld **Paul Herzberg**
Understudy Uri Savir **Rez Kabir**
Yossi Beilin **Jacob Krichefski**
Understudy Terje Rød-Larsen, Thor Bjornevog, US Diplomat,
    Trond Gundersen and German Husband **Jason Langley**
Mona Juul **Lydia Leonard**
Joel Singer **Yair Jonah Lotan**
Ahmed Qurie **Peter Polycarpou**
Trond Gundersen / German Husband / Understudy
    Jan Egeland, Ron Pundak and Joel Singer **Anthony Shuster**
Terje Rød-Larsen **Toby Stephens**
Thor Bjornevog / US Diplomat / Understudy
    Johan Jørgen Holst and Finn Grandal **Daniel Stewart**
Understudy Ahmed Qurie, Hassan Asfour and Yossi Beilin **Allon Sylvain**
Understudy Shimon Peres, Yair Hirschfeld and Joel Singer **Geoffrey Towers**
Johan Jørgen Holst / Finn Grandal **Howard Ward**

Director **Bartlett Sher**
Set Designer **Michael Yeargan**
Costume Designer **Catherine Zuber**
Lighting Designer **Donald Holder**
Sound Designer **Peter John Still**
Projections **59 Productions**
Hair and Wig Designer **Tom Watson**
Casting **Juliet Horsley CDG**
Company Voice Work **Jeannette Nelson**
Dialect Work **Michaela Kennen**
Fight Director **Jonathan Holby**
Associate Director **Oscar Toeman**
Associate Set Designer **Chika Shimizu**
Associate Lighting Designers **Karen Spahn and Alistair Grant**
Costume Supervisor **Deborah Andrews**
Production Manager **Lloyd Thomas**

Opposite page: Lydia Leonard and Toby Stephens
Photograph: Brinkhoff/Mögenburg

In the US

The National Theatre/Headlong production of

People, Places & Things

by **Duncan Macmillan**

Opening St Ann's Warehouse, New York, 25 October 2017

Emma was having the time of her life. Now she's in rehab. Her first step is to admit that she has a problem. But the problem isn't with Emma, it's with everything else. She needs to tell the truth. But she's smart enough to know that there's no such thing. When intoxication feels like the only way to survive the modern world, how can she ever sober up?

Emma **Denise Gough**
T / Ensemble **Jacob James Beswick**
Foster **Alistair Cope**
Jodi / Ensemble **Jacqui Dubois**
Charlotte / Ensemble **Charlotte Gascoyne**
Paul / Dad **Kevin McMonagle**
Mark **Nathaniel Martello-White**
Doctor / Therapist / Mum **Barbara Marten**
Shaun / Ensemble **Himesh Patel**
Laura / Ensemble **Laura Woodward**

Additional Cast **Alexandra Hoover,
Maddison Ridley, Stephanie Sutherland**

Director **Jeremy Herrin**
Set Designer **Bunny Christie**
Costume Designer **Christina Cunningham**
Lighting Designer **James Farncombe**
Music **Matthew Herbert**
Sound Designer **Tom Gibbons**
Video / Projection Designer **Andrzej Goulding**
Movement **Polly Bennett**
Associate Director **Elizabeth Freestone**
Casting **Wendy Spon CDG and Sam Stevenson CDG**
Company Voice Work **Jeannette Nelson and Andrew Wade**

Associate Set Designer **Verity Sadler**
Associate Lighting Designer **Zoe Spurr**
Associate Sound Designer **Alexander Caplen**

Production supported by Areté Foundation / Betsy & Ed Cohen; Leila Maw Straus MBE; Andrew J. Martin-Weber
With additional support from Jon & NoraLee Sedmak; Ellen Foote & Steve Hindy; Remmel Dickinson; Dayna & Brian Lee

Lead International Sponsor Bloomberg Philanthropies

Sponsored by Howard Gilman Foundation

Sponsored by American Express

Opposite page: Denise Gough
Photograph: Teddy Wolff

Hedda Gabler

by **Henrik Ibsen**; in a new version by **Patrick Marber**

Opening This production opened in the Lyttelton Theatre, 12 December 2016. The UK and Ireland tour opened 5 October 2017 at Theatre Royal Plymouth

Just married. Buried alive. Hedda longs to be free… Hedda and Tesman have just returned from their honeymoon and the relationship is already in trouble. Trapped but determined, Hedda tries to control and manipulate those around her, only to see her own world unravel.

Hedda, Tesman's new wife **Lizzy Watts**
Berte, a maid **Madlena Nedeva**
Juliana, Tesman's aunt **Christine Kavanagh**
Tesman, an academic **Abhin Galeya**
Mrs Elvsted, a visitor **Annabel Bates**
Brack, a judge **Adam Best**
Lovborg, a writer **Richard Pyros**

Understudies
Cate Cammack (Hedda Gabler/Mrs Elvsted), **Joseph Capp** (Brack),
JP Conway (Tesman/Lovborg), **Kate Cook** (Juliana/Berte)

Director **Ivo van Hove**
Set and Lighting Designer **Jan Versweyveld**
Costume Designer **An D'Huys**
Sound Designer **Tom Gibbons**
Casting **Sam Stevenson CDG**
Associate Directors **Jeff James and Rachel Lincoln**
Associate Set Designer **Paul Atkinson**
Associate Lighting Designer **Nadene Wheatley**
Associate Sound Designer **Mike Winship**
Fight Director **Bret Yount**
Company Voice Work **Kay Welch**
Assistant Director **Alasdair Pidsley**

Rehearsal Photographer **Ellie Kurttz**
Production Photographers **Brinkhoff/Mögenburg**

Supported by The Williams Charitable Trust

Opposite page: Abhin Galeya and Lizzy Watts
Photograph: Brinkhoff/Mögenburg

On International Tour

The Curious Incident of the Dog in the Night-Time

a new play by **Simon Stephens**; based on the best-selling novel by **Mark Haddon**

Opening Thursday 21 September 2017 at the Royal Theatre Carré, Amsterdam

Christopher, 15 years old, has an extraordinary brain – exceptional at maths while ill-equipped to interpret everyday life. He has never ventured alone beyond the end of his road, he detests being touched and he distrusts strangers. When he falls under the suspicion of killing Mrs Shears' dog, it takes him on a journey that upturns his world.

Christopher Boone **Joshua Jenkins**
Siobhan **Julie Hale**
Ed **David Michaels** / **Stuart Laing**
Judy **Emma Beattie**
Mrs Alexander / Posh Woman / Voice Six **Debra Michaels**
Mrs Shears / Mrs Gascoyne / Voice One / Woman on Train **Amanda Posener**
Roger Shears / Duty Sergeant / Voice Two/Mr Wise / Man Behind Counter / Drunk One **Oliver Boot**
Policeman One / Mr Thompson / Voice Three / Drunk Two / Man with Socks / London Policeman **Matt Wilman**
No 40 / Voice Five / Lady in Street / Information / Punk Girl **Crystal Condie** / **Danielle Kassaraté**
Reverend Peters / Uncle Terry / Voice Four / Station Policeman / Station Guard **Bruce McGregor**
Understudy Judy, Understudy Siobhan, Understudy Mrs Alexander **Emma-Jane Goodwin** / **Emma Keele**
Understudy Roger Shears, Understudy Mr Thompson **Joe Rising**
Understudy Ed, Understudy Reverend Peters **Jâms Thomas** / **Kieran Garland**
Understudy No 40, Understudy Mrs Shears **Danielle Young**
Alternate Christopher **Sam Newton** / **Kaffe Keating**

Director **Marianne Elliott**
Designer **Bunny Christie**
Lighting Designer **Paule Constable**
Video Designer **Finn Ross**
Movement Directors **Scott Graham and Steven Hoggett** for Frantic Assembly
Music **Adrian Sutton**
Sound Designer **Ian Dickinson** for Autograph
Associate Director **Elle While**
Resident Director **Kim Pearce**
Company Voice Work **Charmian Hoare**
Dialect Coach **Jeannette Nelson**
Casting **Jill Green CDG**

Rehearsal Photographer **Alex Rumford**
Production Photographers **Brinkhoff/Mögenburg**

Opposite page: Joshua Jenkins, Matt Wilman and Crystal Condie
Photograph: Brinkhoff/Mögenburg

War Horse

based on the novel by **Michael Morpurgo**; adapted by **Nick Stafford**;
presented in association with the award-winning **Handspring Puppet Company**

Opening The 10th anniversary tour opened at the Marlowe Theatre, Canterbury, 3 October 2017

At the outbreak of World War One, Albert's beloved horse, Joey is sold to the cavalry and shipped to France. Though not yet old enough, Albert joins the army, and embarks on a treacherous mission to find his horse and bring him home.

THE HORSES*
Joey as a foal **Joëlle Brabban, Kiran Landa, Elizabeth Stretton**
Joey head **Tom Stacy** or **Tom Quinn** or **Anna Chessher**
Joey heart **Lewis Howard** or **Domonic Ramsden** or **Chris Charles**
Joey hind **Lucas Button** or **Nicky Cross** or **Samuel Parker**
Topthorn head **Stephen Love** or **Tom Quinn** or **Anna Chessher**
Topthorn heart **Sebastian Charles** or **Domonic Ramsden**
or **Chris Charles**
Topthorn hind **Elan James** or **Nicky Cross** or **Samuel Parker**
Coco **Lucas Button** or **Chris Charles** or **Sebastian Charles**
or **Nicky Cross** or **Lewis Howard** or **Elan James**
or **Domonic Ramsden** or **Samuel Parker**
Heine **Jasper William Cartwright, Simon Victor**
The Goose **Billy Irving**

THE PEOPLE
Chapman Carter / Colonel Strauss **Marcus Adolphy**
John Greig / Dr Schweyk / Sergeant Fine **Adam Barlow**
Friedrich Müller **Peter Becker**
Emilie **Joëlle Brabban**
Billy Narracott / Unteroffizier Klebb **Jasper William Cartwright**
Rose Narracott **Jo Castleton**
Thomas Bone / Veterinary Officer Martin **Jonathan Charles**
Albert Narracott **Thomas Dennis**
Song Man **Bob Fox**
Geordie **Max Gallagher**
Sergeant Allan / Brandt / Soldat Manfred **Chris Garner**
Sergeant Thunder **Andrew Hodges**
Arthur Narracott **William Ilkley**
Lieutenant Nicholls **Ben Ingles**
Johann Schnabel **Billy Irving**
Nurse Annie Gilbert **Kiran Landa**
Ted Narracott **Gwilym Lloyd**
Klausen / Priest **Jack Lord**
David Taylor **Toyin Omari-Kinch**
Paulette **Arinder Sadhra**

Matron Callaghan **Elizabeth Stretton**
Captain Stewart / Ludwig **Simon Victor**
All other parts played by members of the company
* Twelve puppeteers play Joey and Topthorn in rotation at different performances.

Directors **Marianne Elliott and Tom Morris**
Designer / Drawings **Rae Smith**
Puppet Design and Fabrication **Basil Jones and Adrian Kohler**
for **Handspring Puppet Company**
Lighting Designer **Paule Constable**
Director of Movement and Horse Choreography **Toby Sedgwick**
Puppetry Directors **Basil Jones and Adrian Kohler**
Animation & Projection Design **Leo Warner** and **Mark Grimmer**
for **59 Productions Ltd**
Music **Adrian Sutton**
Songmaker **John Tams**
Sound Designer **Christopher Shutt**

For *War Horse* on tour
Revival Director **Katie Henry**
Associate Puppetry Director **Craig Leo**
Resident Director **Charlotte Peters**
Resident Puppetry Director **Matthew Forbes**
Associate Designer **William Fricker**
Associate Costume Designer **Johanna Coe**
Music Director **Tim Sutton**
Music Associate **Matthew Gough**
Associate Lighting Designer **Karen Spahn**
Associate Sound Designer **Rob Bettle**
Associate Projection Designer and Programmer **Emily Malone**
Lighting Associate **George Bach**
Company Voice and Dialect Work **Jacquie Crago**
Fight Director **Paul Benzing**
Casting **Jill Green CDG**

Rehearsal Photographer **Ellie Kurttz**
Production Photographers **Brinkhoff/Mögenburg**

This page:
Members of the company

Photograph:
Brinkhoff/
Mögenburg

Macbeth

by **William Shakespeare** in a new version for teenage audiences by **Justin Audibert and the company**

Opening in a London school, 30 October 2017; touring to schools in London, Doncaster, Sunderland and Wakefield

Amid bloody rebellion and the deafening drums of war, Macbeth and his wife will stop at nothing to fulfil their ambition. Witchcraft, murder, treason and treachery are all at play in this murky world. A bold contemporary retelling of one of Shakespeare's darkest plays.

Macbeth **Nana Amoo-Gottfried**
Lady Macbeth **Shazia Nicholls**
Banquo / Gentlewoman **Stephanie Levi-John**
Macduff **Gabby Wong**
Duncan / 1st Witch / 1st Murderer / Seyton **Adrian Richards**
Lady Macduff / 2nd Witch / Lennox / Surgeon **Tamara Camacho**
Ross / 3rd Witch / Fleance **Johndeep More**
Malcolm / Macduff's son **Kenton Thomas**

Director **Justin Audibert**
Designer **Lucy Sierra**
Composer & Musical Director **Jonathan Girling**
Lighting Designer **Paul Knott**
Sound Designer **Mike Winship**
Fight Director **Kev McCurdy**
Company Voice Work **Rebecca Cuthbertson**
Staff Director **Ruth Mary Johnson**

Production Photographer **Ellie Kurttz**

Partner for Learning: Bank of America Merrill Lynch

Schools Touring is supported by The Mohn Westlake Foundation, The Garfield Weston Foundation, The Ingram Trust, Archie Sherman Charitable Trust, Behrens Foundation, Cleopatra Trust, Allan & Nesta Ferguson Charitable Trust, Jill and David Leuw, Mulberry Trust, The Royal Victoria Hall Foundation and The Robert Gavron Charitable Trust.

Supported by Arts Council's Strategic Touring Fund

Opposite page: Nana Amoo-Gottfried
Photograph: Ellie Kurttz

Supporters

We would like to thank all our supporters for their generous contributions to the National Theatre over the past year.
For more information about supporting the National Theatre, please email support@nationaltheatre.org.uk

Individual Giving

Leadership Gifts

Areté Foundation / Betsy & Ed Cohen
Sir Damon & Lady Buffini
Sir Lloyd & Lady Dorfman
Lawton W Fitt & James I McLaren Foundation
Marcia and Richard Grand
Fondation Hoffmann
Michael Kors & Lance Le Pere
Leila Maw Straus
The Mohn Westlake Foundation
Elizabeth Offord
Mark Pigott KBE
The Sackler Trust
Clive & Sally Sherling
The Thompson Family Charitable Trust
Jacqueline & Richard Worswick
Basil Alkazzi
Celia Atkin
Tom & Sara Attwood
Graham & Joanna Barker
The Broughton Family Charitable Trust
Richard & Samantha Campbell-Breeden
Sabine & Richard Chalmers
Sir Trevor & Lady Chinn
Myoung-Cheul Chung
Remmel Dickinson
Cas Donald
Shawn M Donnelley & Christopher M Kelly
Glenn & Phyllida Earle
The Garvey Family Trust
Kate & Arne Groes
Madeleine Hodgkin
Christopher & Elizabeth Hogbin
Bruce & Suzie Kovner
Stephanie & Carter McClelland
Mactaggart Third Fund
Ian & Beth Mill
Susan Miller & Byron Grote
Mary M Miner
Mirisch and Lebenheim Charitable Foundation
Jordan Roth
Simon & Sue Ruddick
Tim & Cathy Score
Edgar & Judith Wallner
Charlotte & Simon Warshaw
Sian & Matthew Westerman
Marcia B Whitaker
Kathleen J Yoh
and 1 anonymous donor

Olivier Circle

Eric Abraham & Sigrid Rausing
Francis J Aquila
Penny & Bill Bardel
Ginny & Humphrey Battcock
Alex Beard & Emma Vernetti
Cynthia & Ronald Beck
Barbara Broccoli OBE
Julia Brodie
Michael & Mary Carpenter
The Cielinski Family
Peggy Ellis
Peter & Leanda Englander
Robin Geffen
Monica Gerard-Sharp
Richard & Kara Gnodde
Chris & Angela Graham
Ros & Alan Haigh
Lord Roy & Lady Hattersley
Frances Hellman & Warren Breslau
Cathy MacNeil Hollinger & Mark Hollinger
Charles Holloway
Elizabeth & Roderick Jack
Mr & Mrs Jack Keenan
Mark Lee & Ed Filipowski
John & Bridget Macaskill
Christopher & Carol Osborne
Jeff & Liz Peek
Laura Pels
Sara & Paul Phillips
Michael Rose & Roz Rosenblatt
Sir Robin & Lady Saxby
Jon & NoraLee Sedmak
Carol Sellars
David & Sophie Shalit
Richard Sharp
David & Alison Slade
Peter & Esther Smedvig
Francesca Stanfill
Max & Joy Ulfane
Peter Williams & Heather Acton
Alex Wilmot-Sitwell
Anna Wintour
Jody Wolfe
George & Moira Yip
and 5 anonymous donors

Life Benefactors

Eric Abraham & Sigrid Rausing
Access Industries
Irwin & Mary Ackerman
Jonathan & Marie-Claire Agnew
Jeffrey Archer
Celia & Edward Atkin CBE
Royce & Rotha Bell
Ron Beller & Jennifer Moses
Jody Locker Berger
Tony & Gisela Bloom
Keith & Helen Bolderson
Benjamin Bonas
Katie Bradford
Ivor Braka Ltd
Neil & Sarah Brener
The Deborah Loeb Brice Foundation
Jonathan Brooks & Clare Laffin
Russ & Linda Carr
Camilla Cazalet
Terri & Timothy Childs
Sir Trevor & Lady Chinn
Janet M Christensen
Myoung-Cheul Chung
Dr David Cohen CBE
Sir Ronald & Lady Cohen
Ian & Caroline Cormack
Sidney & Elizabeth Corob
Lin & Ken Craig & the Aloisia Hofmann Charitable Trust
Lord Dalmeny
Jose & David Dent
Sir Harry & Lady Djanogly
Edward Dolan-Abrahams
Justin & Emma Dowley
James & Elizabeth Downing
John Drummond
Dame Vivien Duffield DBE
Robyn Durie
David Dutton
Glenn & Phyllida Earle
Ambassador & Edward E Elson
Jane M & Howard D Epstein
Joey Esfandi
John & Jill Fairchild
John & Tawna Farmer
Mr & Mrs Stuart Fiertz
Maureen & Allan Fisher
Lawton W Fitt & James I McLaren Foundation
Emily & Alex Fletcher
Clara & Michael Freeman
Daniel & Joanna Friel
Jacqueline & Michael Gee Charitable Trust
Monica Gerard-Sharp
Jill & Jack Gerber
Mrs Juliet Gibbs
Beth & Gary Glynn
Michael Godbee
Lydia & Manfred Gorvy
Nick & Julie Gould
Michael Grade CBE
Evelyn & David Green
Gabrielle, Lady Greenbury
Jill Hackel & Andrzej Zarzycki
Katherine Hallgarten
Dr Martin Halusa
The Philip & Pauline Harris Charitable Trust
Susan & Richard Hayden
Morven & Michael Heller
The Hintze Family Charitable Foundation
David Hobbs
Dr & Mrs Alan J Horan
Clare & Bernard Horn
Nita Jackson
Lord & Lady Jacobs
Joseph & Jill Karaviotis
Mr & Mrs Jack Keenan
Mathilda & Terence Kennedy Charitable Trust
Gillian & Vimal Khosla
Mark J & Elizabeth L Kogan Charitable Fund
Bruce & Suzie Kovner
The Mark Krueger Charitable Fund
Jon & Mary Leadbetter
Kenneth & Melissa Leet
A Lenson
Lady Lever
Sir Stuart & Lady Lipton
Thomas Lynch
Edward McKinley & Kathleen Lavidge
Justin & Jill Manson
Selina & David Marks
Judy Marshall
Patrick Mears
Mirisch & Lebenheim Charitable Foundation
Carol Mitchell
Miles Morland
Debbie Morris
Mr & Mrs George Newell
Mr & Mrs Jim Nicol
Robert & Jane Norbury
The O'Grady Foundation
Georgia Oetker
Gregory & Susan Palm
Simon & Carolyn Parker Bowles
Barrie & Catherine Pearson
Elizabeth & Daniel Peltz
The Mark Pigott KBE Family
The David & Elaine Potter Foundation
Oliver & Helen Prenn
Quercus Trust
Sue & David Ramsbotham
H K Rausing
Stephen & Monica Richardson
Sir Simon & Lady Robertson
Ruth Robinson
The Roddick Foundation
Bianca & Stuart Roden
Michael Rose & Roz Rosenblatt
Jeffrey A & Marjorie G Rosen
The Michael Harry Sacher Charitable Trust
Theresa Sackler
Anya & John Sainsbury
Yusuf & Fawzia Samad
Jon & NoraLee Sedmak
Carol Sellars
Sir Patrick Sergeant
Dasha Shenkman
Mr & Mrs William Shenkman
Clive & Sally Sherling
Rita & Paul Skinner
Jay & Deanie Stein
Joan Steinberg
Hugh & Catherine Stevenson
Leila Maw Straus
John J Studzinski CBE
Ian Taylor
Eric Tomsett
Jan & Michael Topham
Jonathan Tyler
Mr & Mrs Max Ulfane
The Ury Trust
Edgar & Judith Wallner
Ian & Victoria Watson
Jeffrey Weingarten
Charlotte Weston
Guy Weston
Mary Weston
Susan Wilen
Rachel & Anthony Williams
The Stuart & Hilary Williams Foundation
Sir Robert & Lady Wilson
Dr & Mrs Gerald Woolfson
and 15 anonymous donors

Benefactors

Asli Arah
Philip & Cassie Bassett
Linda Beecham
Ron Beller & Jennifer Moses
Peter & Ali Bennett-Jones
Lord Browne of Madingley
Marty & Michele Cohen
John & Jill Coyle
The Cranshaw Corporation
Guy & Lucy Davison
Alyce Faye Eichelberger-Cleese
Barbara G Fleischman
Emily & Alex Fletcher
Roger & Jane Formby
Adam & Victoria Freudenheim
Paul Friedman & Diane Manley
Mr & Mrs Edward Greene
Uri & Angela Greenwood
Clifford & Sooozee Gundle
Caroline Hoare
Maxine Isaacs
Mrs Philip Kingsley
Christopher Kneale
Khalid Laith
Stephanie & Carter McClelland
Joyce Menschel
Keren Misgav Ristvedt
Andrew & Jennifer Morton
Mr & Mrs A Mosawi
Andrew & Jane Onslow
Clare Parsons
Dr Abe Peled
Clare Rich
Louisa Service OBE
Michael & Melanie Sherwood
Sister Pictures
Marjorie and Michael Stern
Sue & Stuart Stradling
Tozer Family Trust
Diana Venison
Gerry Wakelin
Dr White Williams & Mr Williams
James D Zirin & Marlene Hess
and 2 anonymous donors

Premier Patrons

Lady Alexander of Weedon
Stephen Allcock
Susan Baker & Michael Lynch
Peter Blake-Turner
Michael Bloch
Edward & Victoria Bonham Carter
Léon & Sylvie Bressler
Chris Britton
Simon Burgess
Sir Andrew Cahn
Kate Carpenter & Simon Priddis
Sir Roger & Lady Carr
Adam Chinn
Mary Cirillo-Goldberg
Gill & Garf Collins
Mr & Mrs Paul Collins
Douglas S Cramer & Hugh Bush
Dr Neil Cross
Sir Howard Davies
Dr Elza Eapen & Dr Govindasamy Balachandran
Sir Vernon & Lady Ellis
Don Ellwood & Sandra Johnigan
Maureen Elton
Caryl Englander
Susan Farmer
Kevin Fink
Flavio Feniello
Wendy Fisher
The Edwin Fox Foundation
Ian & Margaret Frost
Johanna & Leslie Garfield
David & Catherine Glickman
Jo-Ann Gregory
Kate Grimond
Charles & Kaaren Hale
Richard H Harding
Pamela, Lady Harlech
Chris & Carolyn Hughes
Sophia Hughes
Jane Hurt
Penny Jackson
William & Weslie Janeway
Ellen & Lewis Kaden
Dr Evi & Dr Costas Kaplanis
Douglas Kennedy
Victor & Gail Khosla
Rupert & Alice King
Herbert Kretzmer OBE
Mr & Mrs T Krumland
David & Linda Lakhdhir
Rocco & Debby Landesman
Steven Larcombe & Sonya Leydecker
Dan & Lucy Lavender
Sir Terry & Lady Leahy
Alan Leibowitz & Barbara Weiss
Norman Leinster
Sarah Lennard
Richard & Claudia Leslie
Marcia Levy
Mark & Sophie Lewisohn
James Libson & Anne Joseph
Leonard & Judith Licht
Rachel Lomax
Dr Sarah McGinty
Donald Main
Audrey Mandela & Sean Phelan
Selina & David Marks
Ian & Serrie Meakins
Aditya Mehta
Brenda Meldrum
Sir Mark & Lady Moody-Stuart
Alice Netter
Stanley Newman & Dr Brian Rosenthal
Emma O'Donoghue
The O'Grady Foundation
Anatol Orient
Mark & Amanda Otway
Carolyn & David Pascall CBE
Kristin M Paulus
Cosima Pavoncelli
Oliver & Emma Pawle
The Porter Foundation Switzerland
William Powar
Tony Randall Theatrical Fund
Gail, Robert & Ian Reichert
Robert Rooney
Pushpinder Saini
Kevin & Carol Sharer
Robert A Silver
Brian D Smith
Helen & Anthony Spiro
Mike Staunton
Tony Stepanski
Anne Sweetbaum
Lady Juliet Tadgell
Simon Tuttle
Gwendolyn van Paasschen
Bruno Wang
Dr Norman E Weeks
Mr & Mrs Brian M Wides
and 5 anonymous donors

Patrons

Mr & Mrs Richard Allan
Tim & Carey Allan
Roger & Angela Allen
Roger Altman & Jurate Kazickas
Joan & Robin Alvarez
Catherine Armitage
Aspect Charitable Trust
James Astor
Annette Atkins & Thomas Joyce
Nancy Austin
Professor John & Carolyn Axford
John Ayton
Jack Bamberger
Mr & Mrs Lawrence Banks
John Barakat & Tracy Lafond Barakat
John Barker
Anne J Barsh
de Baubigny Family
Peter Bazalgette & Hilary Newiss
Arlene Beare
Pamela & Dennis Beck
Sir David & Lady Bell
Ian & Wendelien Bellinger
J & A Bénard
Michael Bennett
Sam & Rosie Berwick
Dr Kate Best
Jewelle & Nathaniel Bickford
Robin & Veronica Bidwell
Mary & Jeffrey Bijur
Mrs Wendy Birkby
The Bertie Black Foundation
Phil Blundell
Mr & Mrs Charlie Bott
John & Jean Botts
Debbie Brayne
Deborah Brett
Elisabeth Bristow
Amy & Adam Brocklehurst
Andrea Brown & Robert M Levande
John & Ruth Bullock
John & Susan Burns
Joan Burstein CBE
Helena Butler
Keith & Pamela Butler-Wheelhouse
Martin Byman & Margaret Samson
Katharine Byrne
Sarah Caplin
Susan Carpenter
Madhvi Chanrai
Fatma Charlwood
Thea Cleminshaw
Tiffany Cloynes
James & Maggie Cochrane
Declan Collier
Mr & Mrs Leigh Collins
Carole & Neville Conrad
A Coombs
Jennifer Coombs
Rosanna Cooper
Victoria Corcoran
Lynette & Robert Craig
Liz Cratchley OBE
Elizabeth Crosoer
Charlotte Cunningham
Kate Dale
Deborah David & Norman A Kurland
Mr & Mrs Jonathan Davie
Dr Genevieve Davies
Merrie L. Davis
Mr & Mrs Ian Hay Davison
Andrew & Gill Dawson
Sir Roger & Lady De Haan
The de Laszlo Foundation
Josephine Dean
Graham & Emma Defries
Scott Delman
David & Jocelyne DeNunzio
Mark Dichter
Dr & Mrs C J Dilloway
Kitty Dinshaw & James Segan
Du Parcq (Jersey) Ltd
Leslie Dubow
Stephen Dunn
Alice Elgart
Tessa Ellis
Sarah Elson
Sue Enoch
Gary Ernest
Davide Erro
Peter & Barbara Esam
Chris Eskdale
Hilary & Rupert Evenett
John & Tawna Farmer
David Fein & Liz Oestreich
Peter Finer
Denys & Victoria Firth
Claire Fisher
Tony Fisher
Mr & Mrs Mortimer Fleishhacker
Susan Fletcher
Ella M Foshay & Michael B Rothfeld
Asmaa El-Kaddar & Dimitrios Fragkiskos
Alan & Valerie Frost
Jonathan Gaisman
Ana Garel-Jones
Jacqueline & Jonathan Gestetner
Piers & Melanie Gibson
Hon William & Lori Gibson
Daniella Gilbertson
The Gillespie Family
Kiki & David Gindler
John & Indrani Gleave
Adam & Carrie Glinsman
M C Godwin
Carolyn Goldbart
Val Gooding & Crawford Macdonald
Paul & Kay Goswell
David Gould
Rt Hon Lord Anthony Grabiner & Lady Grabiner
Lorna Gradden
Alexander Graham
Carolyn Gray
Lesley Gregory
Ann Grieves
Richard & Odile Grogan
Karen Groos
Carol Grose
Robert & Diana Guy
Themy Hamilton
Mr Mark & Dr Moria Hamlin
Sir Michael & Lady Harrison
Maureen & Derek Harte
Samuel A Haubold
Jean Hawkins
Dr Gordon Hay
Lane Heard
Malcolm Herring
The Lady Heseltine
Simon Hessel
Johnny & Jo Hewett
Richard Hicks
Berte Hirschfield
Soo & Jonathan Hitchin
Andrew Hochhauser QC
Sara Holmes-Woodhead
Nicholas Hood
Rodney & Zmira Hornstein
Marc & Isabelle Hotimsky
Angela Howard
Mike & Caroline Howes
Melvyn & Diane Hughes
Inge Hyman
Roda Infield
Simon & Sally Jackson
Emma Jagla
Alison Jenkins & Marc Hayton
Helen Jenkins
Andrew Jenkinson
Jay Johnson & Jonathan Young
Mary Ellen Johnson & Richard Goeltz
Melanie Johnson
Nicholas & Cherry Jones
Brenda Josephs
Ralph & Patricia Kanter
David Kaskel & Christopher Teano
Jutta & Sandeep Katwala
Seamus & Sarah Kelly
David Kelsey
Joy & Geoff Kennard
Stephen & Lynne Kersley
Helene Kessler
David Killick
John Kinder
Roger & Jane Kirby
Frances Kirsh
James Klosty
Bill & Stephanie Knight
David Knox
Latifa Kosta
Christine & Francis Kyle
Kenneth Lamb
David Lanch
Martha Lane Fox
Riki Kane Larimer
Peter Lawrence
Nicola Leach
Shannon Leeman
Jacqueline & Marc Leland
J Leon Charity Fund
Paul Leonard
Karen Lever
Fred M Levin & Nancy Livingston
Troels Levring
Colette & Peter Levy
Lynn Lewis
Robin & Joanna Linnecar
Jeanne Linnes
Sir Sydney Lipworth QC & Lady Lipworth CBE
Lady Lloyd of Berwick
John Lockyer & Jane Creasey
Molly Lowell & David Borthwick
Kathryn Ludlow
Eugene & Carol Ludwig
Angela & Michael Lynch
Felicity Lyons
Ginny Macbeth
Hugh MacDougald
Lisa McGown
Greg & Jane MacLeod
The Maplescombe Trust
Paul & Paula Marber
Frederic Marguerre
Mr & Mrs Jonathan Marks
Lady Medina Marks
Michele Marshall
Peta Martin
Julian & Camilla Mash
Victoria Mather
Jill Matichak
Barbara Minto
Elizabeth & Ashley Mitchell
The Lowy Mitchell Foundation
Barbara Morgan
Mr & Mrs M D Moross
Gary Morris & Robert Venables QC
Allie & Patrick Morrison
Alex & Mai Moss
Gerald Moss
Dr & Mrs Julian Muir
Jimmy Mulville
Mr & Mrs Peter Murray-Smith
Sinead Myerscough
Dr Ann Naylor
Ann & Gavin Neath CBE
Elyse Newhouse
North Street Trust
Sir Charles & Lady Nunneley
Midge & Simon Palley
Kathrine Palmer
Lord & Lady Pannick
Jackie Parker
Tim Parker
Michael & Mary Parkinson
Dalip & Chandrika Pathak
Judy Peck
Jane A. Peterson & Paul A. Kaju
Gordon & Marian Pell
Roger & Virginia Phillimore
Richard Phillips
Sir Stephen & Lady Phillips
Murray Pickering
David Pike
Paulita Pike
Gilbert E Pilgram
Anne & Barry Pinson
Andrew Pitt
Pat & John Porter
Mr & Mrs Michael Pragnell
Marie Prutton
Trevor Pugh
JP Rangaswami
Greg & Karen Reid
Nick Reid
Christopher Marek Rencki
Joyce Reuben
His Honour Michael Rich QC
Caroline Roboh
David Rocklin
Barbara Rogers
Kristina Rogge
Richard & Mary Rosenberg
Tim Rosenberg
Sue & Tony Rosner
Diana Ross
Jon & Susan Rotenstreich
Peter Roth
David Royds
M Rubens
The Ruddock Foundation for the Arts
William & Hillary Russell
Betsy & Jack Ryan
William & Julie Ryan
John & Jeremy Sacher Charitable Trust
Susan Sachs Goldman
Richard & Virginia Salter
Anthony & Sally Salz
Ruth & Brian Sandelson
Michael Sayers QC
Michael & Beth Schneider
Peter Scott
Philippa Seal & Philip Jones QC
Eileen Serbutt
Hazel Shanken
Mr & Mrs Mark Shanker
Ellen & Dan Shapiro
Russ Shaw & Lesley Hill
Dr Lorri Sills
Anthony Simpson & Susan Boster
Andrea Sinclair & Serge Kremer
Phyllis Singer
Frank & Mary Skillern
Sylvia Slifka
Kate Sloane
Francis & Jenny Small
Christopher & Ingeborg Smallwood
Mr & Mrs R A H Smart
John & Ann Smith
Tessa Smith
Sir Harry & Lady Solomon
Howard Solomon & Sarah Billinghurst Solomon
Claire Stansfield
Kathryn Steinberg
George & Elizabeth Stevens
Gill Stewart
Judy & David Stewart
Lindsey Stewart
Oliver & Sally Stocken
Olive & Michael Stone
Siân Stonehill
Maria & Julian Sturdy-Morton
Andrew & Laura Sukawaty
Sir John & Lady Sunderland
Tobias Svensson
Robert & Patricia Swannell
Esther & Romie Tager QC
Bernard & Nadine Taylor
Lucie Tepla
Chantal Thompson
Ian Tollett
Sara & Nigel Tozzi
Mr & Mrs John C Tucker
Christopher & Julia Tugendhat
Margaret K B Turner
Christina Turton
Sharon Tyler
Jeffrey & Laurie Ubben
Dominic & Amanda Vail
Marina Vaizey
Maria Vecchiotti
Peter Ventress
Mr & Mrs Eric Vezie
Donna Vinter
Frank & Emily Vogl
Mr & Mrs Jeffrey Walker
Lucy Walsh Waring
Andrew Walters
Jan Warner
Stephen & Sophie Warshaw
Denie & Frank Weil
Nicholas Wells
Geoff Westmore
Ailsa White
Graham & Sue White
Olga White
Jill Whitehouse
Anne-Marie Williams
Beth Williams
Marilyn & Geoffrey Wilson

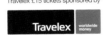
NT Future

We would like to thank everyone who has supported the NT Future capital campaign, with particular gratitude to the major donors listed below:

Personnel of the National Theatre

BOARD
Sir Damon Buffini (Chair)
Kate Mosse (Deputy Chair)
Dame Ursula Brennan DCB
Sabine Chalmers
Sir Lenny Henry

Vikki Heywood CBE
Elizabeth Offord
Alan Rusbridger
Tim Score
Simon Warshaw

DIRECTOR
Rufus Norris

EXECUTIVE DIRECTOR
Lisa Burger

ASSOCIATES
Paul Arditti
Paule Constable
Dominic Cooke
Nadia Fall
Simon Godwin

Kobna Holdbrook-Smith
Katrina Lindsay
Tom Morris
Lyndsey Turner

DEPUTY ARTISTIC DIRECTOR
Ben Power

ASSOCIATE PRODUCER
Christine Gettins

AUDIENCES & MARKETING
Alex Bayley

CHIEF OPERATING OFFICER
Liz Fosbury

COMMERCIAL & MEDIA
Colin Lawrence

DEVELOPMENT
Kathryn Marten

HUMAN RESOURCES
Tony Peers

INFORMATION TECHNOLOGY
Jon Cheyne

LEARNING
Alice King-Farlow

NT PRODUCTIONS
Kash Bennett

PRODUCTION
Paul Handley

TECHNICAL
Jonathan Suffolk

ASSOCIATE CONSULTANT PRODUCER
Pádraig Cusack

CASTING
Alastair Coomer CDG

MUSIC
Marc Tritschler

NEW WORK
Emily McLaughlin

NT AMERICA
Tim Levy

VOICE
Jeannette Nelson

DEPUTY ENTERPRISES DIRECTOR
George Cardwell

EXTERNAL RELATIONSHIPS & PARTNERSHIPS
John Langley

GENERAL COUNSEL
Peter Taylor

PUBLISHING
Harry Scoble

ARCHIVE
Erin Lee (Head)
Jennie Borzykh
Frances Horner
Sophie Jump
Matthew McFrederick
Malcolm Mathieson

AUDIENCES & MARKETING
Becky Wootton (Deputy Director of Audiences & Marketing)
Box Office
Aidan O'Rourke (Head)
Clare Amos
Tony Bannister
Holly Barbour
Sophie Beckwith
Naomi Bowen
James Broderick (Systems Mgr)
Alasdair Carson-Sheard (Operations Mgr)
Zachary Danvers
Angela Eyton
John Etherington
Brandon Force
Henry Francis
Laura Glover
Josephine Grosset
Daniel Harlock
Sheryl Hill
Melanie Hilton (Sales Mgr)
Kyle Jarvis
Rob Kerr
Mia Kosminsky
William Lee
Stephanie Lodge
Katie-Ann McDonough
Fabiana Palladino
Aine Pullan
Andrew Reid
Lucy Robinson
Christine St Fort

Lauren Shields
Cameron Slater
Nicholas Southwell
Ross Virgo
Corie Xavier
Edward Yelland
Graphic Design Studio
Ollie Winser (Creative Director)
Billy Bull
Jen Dennis
Rebecca Eborall
Bastian Mueller
Louise Richardson
Elliot Wilkinson
Marketing
Ali Forbes (Head of Marketing Campaigns)
Emma Power (Head of Strategic Marketing Projects)
Rishi Coupland (Head of Data Intelligence)
Charlotte Cosgrove
Thanos Gkofas (Senior Data and Insight Manager)
Yasmeen Ismail
Christopher Jones
Aurora Lewis
Sean McParland
Ludmila Neto
Karen Palmer
Tara Parashar
Laura Sangster-Poole
Dilshad Shawki
Thom Wallis
Katie A Williams
CASTING
Juliet Horsley CDG
Bryony Jarvis-Taylor
Isabella Odoffin
Jacob Sparrow
Sam Stevenson CDG (Deputy)

COMMERCIAL & MEDIA
Broadcast
Nellie Alston
Ieva Bachtiarova
James Bowen
Flo Buckeridge
George Bushaway
Jim Cross
Dawn Davis
Miranda Ford
James Foster
Tom Gill
Joanna Green
Stephanie Hall
Phil Horton
Jamie Isbell
Louise King
Claire Lester
Kate Moore
Colin Pearce
Emma Reidy
Jessica Richardson
Gareth Roberts
Jasmine Sandalli
Hannah Sayer
Sam Sedgman
Richard Tanner
James Thompson
Digital Development
Toby Coffey (Head)
Christian Bravo
Matt Crinion
Tuyet Huynh
Roderick Morgan
Johanna Nicholls
COMMERCIAL OPERATIONS
Audience Experience
Gabriela Gandolfini (Director of AE)
Geraldine McCormick
Samantha Harding
Sharon Salihu
Andrew Skipper
Catering
Neil Brooke

Simon Flint (Executive Chef)
Luke Addis
Lydia Addo
Szilvia Agacz
Stefan Agnew
Tareic Alphonse
Csaba Ambrus
Chantelle Amon
Paul Amondu
Anyebe Anteyi
Millie Arnott
Rianna Ash
Holly Ashman
Eve Atkinson
Alessio Atzori
Omar Austin
Assane Ba
Malgorzata Bachniak
Thomas Baker
Jordan Bangura
Ashleigh Barice
Daniel Bell
Jessica Bell
Emma Bentley
Troy Berley
Nicola Bernardelle
Lauren Bevan
Zoe Biles
Jasmine Blackburn
Alexander Bloomer
Polis Butkus
Joe Bence
Carl Blades
Millie Boardman
Robert Boulton
Juste Brazenaite
Rebecca Brough
Paige Broughton
Paul Brown
Susanna Buckle
Matthew Burns
Alexsandrs Caciks
Thomas Campion
Rebecca Carewe-Jeffries
Lucy Carpenter
Zena Carswell

Tim Chapman
Flora Charlton
Alexandr Chilovati
Charlotte Churm
Bartosz Chylak
Simone Ciminelli
Lauren Clancey
Michael Clarke
Jade Clulee
Joseph Coates
Joseph Cocklin
Ilona Cofalska
Radoslaw Cofalski
Arthur Cole
Tyler Conti
Sarah Corbin
Meghan Cosgrove
Jon Cotterell
Michael Cottrell
Calvin Crawley
Claire Crossley
Nailah Cumberbatch
Carla Cunha-Tosta
Thomas Cunningham
Alieu Darboe
Edesio Da Silva
Lowri Ann Davies
Jodi Davis
Kieran Dean
Marcin Debski
David Del Peral Juarez
Abdoul Dia
Miguel Diaz
Leonardo Di Renzo
Mor Penda Diop Niang
Sula Douglas-Folkes
Iva Dukova
Leah Duxbury
Asfraf Ejjbair
Imane El Bakkali
Mohammed El Bakkali
Sara El Bakkali
Sara Erkleiv
Cecile Farber
Jesus Fernandez
Andre Fialho
Jacqueline Fisher
Jasmyn Fisher-Ryner

Sarah Flanagan
Timothy Fraser
Jose Carlos Freitas Da Silva
Tanya Fryer
Leah Gaffrey
Anna Gallo
Stefania Gallo
Neil Gardner
Maeve Garner
Tarcisio Garozi
Chelsey George
Leah Georges
Arami Gimenez
Jonathan Glick
Duarte Gomes
Juliana Goncalves Da Silva
Anita Gonzalez
Nesah Gonzales
Aaron Gordon
Natalie Graham
Catriona Granger
Osmond Grant
Darcy Gresley
Wesley Griffith
Rachel Grubb
Bartosz Grzelak
Oliver Gyani
Daniel Haswell
Seabert Henry
Beatriz Hernandez Gazquez
Stephanie Hill
Hannah Hodge
Hollie Hodgson
Christine Holland
Laura Hopwood
MacKensie Horn
Andrew Horton
Severine Howell-Meri
Lindsey Huebner
Natasha Hutchinson
Richard Igoe
Charlotte Ive
Syreeta Jacca
Nicholas Jackson
Arabella Jacobson

Segun Jaiyeola
Martha Jamal
Kamila Janicka
Dariusz Jendrusiak
Georgina Jones
Kieran Jones
Serge Kabongo
Katherine Kehoe
Alice Kiff
Robert Killalea
Richard Kirjak
Miroslaw Kobosz
Andrea Kovacs
Alex Kristoffy
Robin Kristoffy
Aleksejs Kulikovskis
Suleiman Kwesikwa
Courtney Larkin
Steven Laverty
Robert Leach
Lajos Legrady
Claire Leith
David Lenik
Siyianoi Leteyio
Lauren Lewis
Mauricia Lewis
Katherine Le Witt
Giovana Lorensatto
Vladimir Lupan
Paul McAleer
Alish McCormick
Timothy McFarland
Grant McIntyre
Sophie McKay
Ian Mairs
Medea Manaz
Edie Maniata
Gabriel Marras
Luke Marsden
Myles Marshall
Fernando Martinez Benito
Zanna Mercer
Gunta Mijere
Lucy Miller
Marina Mondalska
Juan Francisco Montero Garcia

Matthew Morrison
Maria Morrone
Oliver Mortimer
Stephen Moseley
Jay Mullinger
Lewis Newman
Oliver Nicholas
Valerie Nkwo
Thomas Nunez
Chioma Nwalioba
Joseph O'Malley
Hubert Omanski
Luke Orrin
Maedb Orsborn-Fitchie
Katie Overstall
Gabriel Owen
Meshack Owira
Samson Oyelakin
Sydrik Paderes
Bela Palinkas
Sinead Parker
Jessica Parker Humphreys
Christine Paul
Jiri Navratil
Emily Needham
Yin Le Phyo
Ciara Power
Charlotte Priestley
Chiara Raicovi
Alexandre Ramos
Luis Ramos
Jasmine Raymond
Joel Renouf
Lucie Richards-Cottell
Cal Robertson
Callum Robertson
Rebecca Robinson
Adriana Rodrigues De Almeida
Sabrina Roett
Dominic Rose
Phillip Rouse
Artur Ruman
Caroline St Quinton
Jacob Salihu
Xenia Salihu
Demipreet Sandhu

Sussan Sanii
Carlo de los Santos
Mario Savaris
Pauline Schena
Segolene Scheuer
Bogdan Scutariu
Olivia Seaton-Hill
Mikhail Sen
Arvids Senkans
Gabor Seregely
Ursula Seruga
Amelia Sharp
Freya Sharp
Lewis Shaw
Michael Shon
Beatriz Sidgman Gutierrez
Paulina Sidhom
Agnieszka Sidor
Tomas Simecek
Samuel Sims
Tristan Smith-Morris
Laura Smithers
Antigoni Spanou
Jamie Spindlove
Sergejs Strogonous
Humera Syed
Cassia Symes
Csilla Szabo
Evelina Tamulionyte
Dayana Tellerias
Barbara Thomas
Faye Thomas
James Thorpe-Woods
Patrik Toman
Alex Torrijos Conde
Issouf Toure
Jon Traynor
Leyton Turner
Davy Tyler
Christopher Underhay
Yuliana Vajzovic
Michael Van Der Put
Aleksander Vasilev
Gabor Ver
Ben Victor
Hannah Victory
Sophie Waghorn

Lauren Waine
Daisy Watford
Amy Watkins
Zoe Watson
Peter Watts
Holly Whinney
Chris Wilby
Thomas Wilby
Sophie Wilkinson
Simon Williams
Ryan Wilson
Abdul Yeboah
Daniel Yelland
Stoil Yurukov
Lukasz Zablocki
Aleksandrs Zalmans
Stephanie Zarasate
Monsaf Zermani
Harriet Ziebell
Aleksandra Zylinska
Commercial Operations Finance
Vicente Casana Arguis
Jade Golloghly
Jan Humphries
Sarah Kamran
Chance Mauluka
Hospitality Events
Ali Blows (Head of Commercial Events & (Business Development)
Harvey Bassett
Niamh Blackman
Elliot Bornemann
Felicia Boshorin
Fleur Burrows-Jones
Neil Clarke
Elizabeth Fenn
Tunde Garrison
Neil Gordon
Katherine Hearst
Megan Philip
Benjamin Szuts
Helen Thomas
Shahail Woodcock
Karolina Zatorska

House Management
Stephen Hayes (Head)
Olivia Caussanel
Jay Hannaford
Nicholas Huggins
Jacky Masson
Brigitte Adela
Aisha Ajona
Carla Almeida
Jessica Aro
Evelyn Arrais
Kirsty Ayers
Ross Barnes
Abigail Bates
Stuart Benson
Jack Blundell
Rhys Bowden
Annabelle Broad
Jonathan Brown
Julian Bruton
Ian Burr
Dejan Butler
Owen Bywater
Andrew Candish
Katriona Chapman
Richard Charlton
Holly Clark
Jo Clark
Emily Collinson
Stephanie Compton
Victor Correia
Paul Davies
Gail Deacon
Lucy Dobson
Marina Dumchera
Robert Edmonds
Sian Edwards
Antonia Elson-Clayton
Richard Fathers
Annette Franklin
Iain Gibbons
Joshua Gough-Yate
Susan Gregory
Alex Grey
Megan Griffith
Shona Guha
Kieran Hamm-Pascoe
Miranda Heath
Madhia Hussain
Ese Ighorae
Callum King
Sage Lancaster
Reuben Lane
Keith Lawson
Matthew Leonard
Jasmin Mandi-Ghomi
Maria Marinova
Fred Mead
Marcio De Melo
Edward Mosse
Alice Osmanski
Connie Owen
Elodie Pasqualini
Albert Pizzaia
Marilii Saar
Dinesh Sattee
Russell Saunders
Lily-Josephine Sims
Kathryn Sketchley
Rosalyn Slater
Marsha Solon
Cassie Solon-Parry
George Staines
John Staveley
Richard Stevens
Lorianne Tika-Lemba
Paige Tribe
Jennifer Tyler
Thomas Ward
Janet Worster
Victoria Wright

Retail
Kate Bone (Head)
Carla Almeida
Eve Atkinson
Zena Carswell
Tom Dykes
Carrie Hill
Madhia Hussain
Gavin Innes
Charlotte Ive
Paulina Kominiak
Molly McNerney
Lucy Miller
Juliet Okotie
Dana Olarescu
Christopher Roberts
Michael Ross
Michael van der Put
Benjamin Victor
Richard Woolley

Stage Door
Vincent Hawkins
Cathy Miller
Linda Tolhurst

Support Services
Chris Snow (Head)
Emmanuel Adedeji
Stephen Ayodele
Daniel Bowater
Felix Briant
Richard Carey
Tim Dare
Kerry Hunt
Louise Kilden
Joshua King
Guglielmo Lanzilli
Michael McInerney
Dave Mulcrone
Jonathan Mulcrone
Joana Pereira
Alexander Rybinski
Saleena Saeed
Dean Smith
Mark Smith
Jamie Spooner
Gary Tigwell
Emeka Ugwuanyi
Stewart Upson
Ovomor Urumedji
Henry Williams

Tours & Visiting
Alison Rae (Head)
Sophie Askew
Rupert Hatton
Maya Jani
Emily Jenik
Jessica Jones
Jack McDougall
Matthew Patterson

COMMUNICATIONS
Emily Newton
Duncan Watt

COMPANY MANAGEMENT
Gemma Tonge (Head)
Mary Carter (Company Administration Mgr)
Janice Heyes (Deputy Head of Company Management)
Hannah Horsburgh (Company & Music Administrator)

Stage Management
Fiona Bardsley
Ian Connop
Ben Donoghue
Ian Farmery
Nik Haffenden
Anna Hill
David Marsland
Jo Nield
Alison Rankin
Andrew Speed
Jane Suffling
Ruth Taylor
Shane Thom

DEVELOPMENT
Matt Armstrong
Harprit Bhogal
Emily Birden
Frances Bridgewater
Rachel Clarke Ederle
Maire Dallamore
Paris Faro
Emily Fuller
Hannah Griffith
Kathryn Hardy
Claire Heaney
Daniel Hewitt
Alison Howard
Georgia Ingham
Ellie Lambert
Ruth Naylor
Kavina Nijjar
Natalie Panto
Cressida Peever
Anna-Fleur Rawlinson
John Rodgers (Consultant)
Isobel Shipp
Kieran Skelton
Chanel Srisung
Charlotte Surman
Dominique Trotter
Jess Twumasi
Dagmar Ulrich
Hamble Wallace
Lindsay Walker
Jemma Wark
Sarah Woods
Lauren Young

DIRECTORS' OFFICE
Donna Parker (Board Secretary)
Lao Lee
Faye Merralls
Rachel Powell
Cameron Slater

EXTERNAL RELATIONSHIPS & PARTNERSHIPS
Ros Hayes (Head of Access)

FINANCE & GOVERNANCE
Angela McDermott (Deputy Finance Director)
Ese Adjekughele
Louise Boyd
Charlotte Doherty
James French
Lorraine Ganney
Ester Goemans
Safron Grothier
Kim Hooper
Glynis Hunte
Olga Jarosh
Ruth McCabe
Lee McKay
Charles Mapo
Gina Mavraki
Christine Murray
Lynne O'Hara
Anselm Onyenani
Lotte Pople Hoskins
Yllka Sopa
Guy Thomas
Catherine Williamson

HUMAN RESOURCES
Rachel Saxon (Deputy Director of HR)
Gemma Baxter (Workforce Development Mgr)
Charlotte Bevan (Diversity Associate)
Elaine Chapman
Ayesha Fatima
Kathryn Geraghty (Workforce Development Mgr)
Alex Jean-Baptiste
Kate Lovelock
Rebecca Merriman
Phoebe Pickard
Natalie Roberts
Heather Rowe
Neena Shea
Danuta Trestka

Medical/Welfare
Yve Corkett-Mayana OHN
Juliet Messenger (Welfare Counsellor)
Lucy Walsh OHN
Dr Laurence Gerlis (Medical Adviser)

INFORMATION TECHNOLOGY
Emiliano Borselli
Philip Carter
Maurice Evans
Lisa Guy
Mark Hands
Lee-Anne Inglis
Ruby Iqbal
Stan Liu
Nicholas Martin
Matt Miles
Mike Murtagh
Tom Rhodes
Mel Shead
Beryl Taylor
Spencer Trim-West
George Tunnicliffe
Karen Williams

LEARNING
Paula Hamilton (Deputy Director of Learning)
Ola Animashawun
Holly Aston
Jane Ball
Perri Blakelock
Oliver Branton
Sheila Chawla
Elizabeth Coates
Sophie Cornell
Hannah Cox
Róisín Devine
Rio Dunsdon-Fry
Sarah Eastaff
Adele Geddes
Jack Heaton
Alexandra Hensby
Rebecca Jeetoo
Nadia Lakhani
Virginia Leaver (General Manager)
Lorna McGinty
Judith Merritt (Head of Talks and Exhibitions)
Alicia Mills
Samantha Moore
Ella Murdoch
Jenna Omeltschenko
Flo Paul
Andrew Pritchard
Ali Rich
Jackie Tait

MAJOR PROJECTS
Anna Anderson (Head of Major Projects)
Holly Dickson
Jessica Johnson
Ciara McNeely
Mark Scott
Paul Jozefowski (Head of Building Design & Environmental Sustainability)

NEW WORK
Rachel Twigg (Senior New Work Mgr)
Oladipo Agboluaje (Writer in Residence)
Lyndon Baines
Sarah Clarke
Katy deMain
Nick Flintoff
Gillian Greer
Matt Harrison
Patrick Hughes
Beth Nesbitt
Stewart Pringle
Josh Scuse
Nina Steiger
Alexander Zeldin (Peter Hall Resident Director Award)

NT PRODUCTIONS
Amelia Anderson
Jack Bull
Jason Culverwell
Heather Epple
Debbie Farquhar
Abigail Fisher
Thea Foster
Sarah Hunt
Zak Khan
Lauren King
Akosua Koranteng
Susie Newbery
Chris O'Quinn
Damian Partington
Sarah Quinn
Rachel Roussel-Tyson
Milo Spence
Martina Thompson
Molly Twiselton

PRESS
Ruth Greenwood (Head of Press – Interim)
Rhian Bennett
Emma Hardy
Elaine Jones
Mary Parker
Louisa Terry

PRODUCING & PLANNING
Vicky Hawkins (Head of Producing)
Jo Hornsby (Head of Planning)
Anna Cole (Scheduling & Designers' Contracts Mgr)
Laura Glover (Producing Coordinator)
Jack Hudson (Planning Administrator)
Fran Miller (Project Producer)
Suzy Morgan (Producing Coordinator)
Rachel Quinney (Project Producer)
Claire Sclater (Literary Contracts Manager)
Sarah Stott (Scheduling Coordinator)

Music
Roman Benedict
Terry Eldridge (Music Producer)
Matthew Scott (Consultant)

PRODUCTION
Frances Dawes (Production Office Mgr)
Serena Basra (Production Assistant)

Production Managers
Anna Anderson
Anthony Newton
Tariq Rifaat

Deputy Production Managers
Michael Ager
Vivienne Clavering
Tom Lee
Richard Eustace

Projects & Events Production
Jonny Ward (Head)
Helen Donnelly

Production Design Assistants
Niall McKeever
Grace Venning

PUBLISHING
Sarah Corke
Charles Meyrick
Hannah Phillips

SAFETY
Jennifer Mulgrew-Smith (Head)
Georga Costi
Holly Dickson
Cassie McCallin
Anisha Sood

SECURITY
Darren Cresswell (Head)
Peter Deacon
Trevor Fenn
Collen Heskey
Gordon Nicholson
Jamie Thomas

TECHNICAL

Armoury & Special Effects
Paul Wanklin (Head of Armoury & SE)

Automation
Jay Bruce
Joanne Colley
Adam Fretwell
David Helyar (Automation Control Mgr)
Duncan Weir (Stage Automation Mgr)

Costume
Carol Lingwood (Head)

Costume Production
Iona Kenrick (Deputy)
Aimee Carter
Clare Carter
Elizabeth Rose Crossman
Barbara Fuchs
Caite Goodwin
Jacqui Hamer
Reuben Hart
Nicola Herlihy
Sarah Holmes
Ashley Holtom
Liz Honeybone
Victoria King
Cat Ladd
Sarah Mercer
Tony Rutherford
Claire Suckall
Emma Sunley
Sharon Williams
Faye Young

Costume & Props Hire
Elizabeth Murray (Hire Department Mgr)
Holly Hobbs (Deputy)
Sarah Baker
Guy Goodbody
Anthony Harrison
Suzanne Hickinbotham
Anthony Kelly
Stephanie Laing
Paul Rofe
Linda Walsh
Sara Wan

The Drawing Office
Alan Bain (Head)
Tom Atkinson
Jef Gage
Suzanne Hickinbotham
Natalie McCormack
Emma Morris
Emma Pile
Daniel Radley-Bennett
Janet Williamson
John Winters

Facilities
Tim Kingston (Head)
John Baginsky
Keith Batchelor
Paul Blackmore
Andrea Bottaro
Natalie Chambers
Stephen Douglas
Robert Hopkins
Anthony Howell
Robert Hunt
Ron Jackson
Kevin Jones
Denis McCormick
Joseph Pegram
Brian Picton
Sebastian Powderham-Rattan
Daniel Proctor
Paul Sayer
Mark Ward
Ross Williams

Lighting
Matt Drury (Head)
Paul Hornsby (Lighting Resources Mgr)
Daniel Murfin (Lighting Control Mgr)
Marc Williams (Lighting Operations Mgr)
Karin Anderson
Breandan Ansdell
Briony Berning-Pollard
Neill Berning-Pollard
Neville Billmoria
Henri Charlton
Laura Choules
Laurence Clayton
Gareth Connoley
Steve Dart
Nick Di Gravio
Jerome Douglas
Jane Dutton
Jess Faulks
Rachael Finney
Kate Greaves
Clara Halse
Michael Harpur
Chris Harris
Chris Howells
Amy Jonas
Paul Knott
Tony Lewis
Huw Llewellyn
Nathan Long
James Lye
Dave McMaster
Jerome Moran-Seekings
Tamykha Patterson
Katie Pitt
Olivia Richardson (Technical Apprentice)
Kelsey Smith (Technical Apprentice)
Jeremy Turnbull
Craig West
Nadene Wheatley
Jack Williams
Jahmare Williams-Wright (Technical Apprentice)
Alex Varlow

Props
Nicky Holderness (Head)
Michael Garrett (Workshop Mgr)
Kirsten Shiell (Senior Prop Supervisor)
Eleanor Smith (Senior Prop Supervisor)
Steve Dart
Abi Duddleston
Bruce Dunning
Allan Edwards
Wendy Hall
Joe Harvey
Rebecca Johnston
Catherine Kapff
Chris Lake
Michelle McLucas
Tracey Russell
Lara Scott
Jamie Tait
Jess Walsh
Sian Willis

Rigging & Scenic Logistics
Kieran Gonzalez
Jim Harlow
Phil Horsburgh
Neill Shimmen
Riche Tarr
Matthew Wheeler

Scenic Construction & Scenic Art
Kate John (Interim Head of Construction)
Gavin Gibson (Head of Scenic Art)
Ken Rose (Head of Carpentry & Metalwork)
Joel Baldwin (Apprentice)
Sophie Barrett (Apprentice)
Stephen Brown
Ian Cooper
Dave Cotton
Charles Court
Daina Ennis
Jen Espley
Tim Fawcett
Amanda Green (Scenic Construction Project Coordinator)
Clayton Handley
Colin Humphries
Sarah Kier
Cass Kirchner
Alan McCabe
Sophie Naylor (Apprentice)
Barrie Nield
Glen Pew
David Price
Paul Sheppard
Paul Smith
Lindsay Tuffnell

Scenic Logistics
Andrew Ormesher (Scenic Logistics Mgr)
Trevor Joseph

Sound & Video
Dominic Bilkey (Head)
Sarah Black (Deputy Head)
Suzanne Diakun (Co-ordinator)
Matt Berry
Mogzi Bromley-Morgans
Clive Bryan
Alex Caplen
Charlie Foran
Angela Gomez-Pulido
Elayne Hall
Gemma Harrison
Chris Jackson
Jack Lord
Kyle Macpherson
Jamie McIntyre
Javier Pando
Joel Price
Jonas Roebuck
Claire Stamp
Rosie Stroud
Alex Twiselton
Ben Vernon
Sarah Weltman
Vicky Wilkinson

Sound & Video Resources
Gurjit Dhinsa (Mgr)
Elena Chrysopoulou
Clark Henry-Brown
Gavin Marrable
Richard Moores
Ben Steinitz

Stage
Gary Pell (Head)
Simon Godfrey (Deputy)
Kevin Theobald (Mgr)
Mark Adams
Patricia Andreucci
Roy Bernard
Richard Booth
Suresh Chawla
Bob Cross
Michael Day
Richard Gosling
Alan Gribben
Danny Halsey
Lee Harrington
Shane Hover
Iain Jolly
David Malaley
Martin Mardon
Danny O'Neill
Pradip Pankhania
Barry Peavot
Ken Pedersen
Simon Pink
Jamie Powell
Yuri Queiroz
Jody Robinson
Alex Self
Gary Tolhurst
Dave Tuff
Will Watson
Karen Wychgel

Stage Engineering
Michael Lane (Head)
David Dargie
Darren Middleditch
Bryn Oram

Technical Administration
Fiona Oram (Tech Admin Mgr)
Annie Eves-Boland
Susanna Keeley (Stages Admin)
Sally Roy (Workshops Admin)
Hannah Sadler (Costume & W, H&M Admin)
Olivia Sangster-Bullers (Lighting Administrator & Co-ordinator)
Lucy Tory

Wardrobe
Michael Roff (Head)
Helen Bermingham
Laura Clarke
Jess Dixon
Paulina Domaszewska
Ben Edmonds
Samantha Hadfield
Jo Kühn
Katie Lawman
Jo Lusted
Julie Burns McKenzie
Michelle MacMillan
Louise Marchand-Paris
Philippa Mawbey
Carly Millard
Ralph Mills
Michelle Rodda
Amanda Tyrell
Elize Van Velden
Steve Walker
Ruth Williams

Wigs, Hair & Make-up
Giuseppe Cannas (Head)
Helen Casey (Deputy)
Kathryn Adams
Daisy Beer
Gillian Blair
Sophie Bowerman
Adele Brandman
Jean Carlos De Bias Moreno
Renata Hill
Kim Kasim
Leanne Lashbrook
Gabrielle Mason
Fiona Matthews
Megan Norris
Leah O'Connell (Apprentice)
Sarah Lou Packham
Laura Romain
Suzanne Scotcher
Natalie Shephard

THE AMERICAN ASSOCIATES OF THE NATIONAL THEATRE
Mary Angelo
Meghan Cooper
Quinn Corbin
Kirsten Hughes
Elana Lantry

NT AMERICA
Francesca De La Vega

The National Theatre is grateful for the work of its staff, freelancers and volunteers, past and present.